Justice Is Served

*How And Why Christian Culture
Inherently Supports Veganism*

D1563683

WITHDRAWN

By Brad Johnson

Bonus Gift

Dear *Justice Is Served* readers,

As a thank you for picking up a copy of the book I'd like to give you one of my Top 15-Selling Kindle books, *Lose Fat Rapidly*, free...

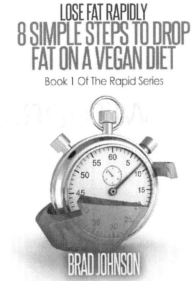

To obtain your free copy just go here:
http://rapidseries.s3.amazonaws.com/Lose+Fat+Rap idly+V4.pdf

Who Is This Book For?

This book is for:

- Anyone who is curious about veganism
- Anyone who is wondering how veganism and Christianity are related
- Anyone who is interested in the topic of justice
- Vegans who are interested in seeing how Christianity connects to their diet and lifestyle
- Christian vegans or vegetarians who are looking to persuade others of the logic and viability of their lifestyle/diet/choices

Who Is This Book Not For?

This book is not for anyone who is assuming or hoping they'll find every answer to all their questions in one book. This is not for people who are trying to disprove veganism or Christianity. This book is not for anyone expecting a light read. This book is not for those primarily interested in the dietary/nutrition side of veganism (I have written other books on the subject).

"Why this frenzy of sacrifices?"
GOD'S asking.
"Don't you think I've had my fill of burnt sacrifices,
rams and plump grain-fed calves?
Don't you think I've had my fill
of blood from bulls, lambs, and goats?
When you come before me,
whoever gave you the idea of acting like this,
Running here and there, doing this and that—
all this sheer *commotion* in the place provided for
worship?

13-17 "Quit your worship charades.
I can't stand your trivial religious games:
Monthly conferences, weekly Sabbaths, special
meetings—
meetings, meetings, meetings—I can't stand one
more!

"Meetings for this, meetings for that. I hate them!
You've worn me out!
I'm sick of your religion, religion, religion,
while you go right on sinning.
When you put on your next prayer-performance,
I'll be looking the other way.
No matter how long or loud or often you pray,
I'll not be listening.
And do you know why? Because you've been tearing
people to pieces, and your hands are bloody.
Go home and wash up.
Clean up your act.
Sweep your lives clean of your evildoings
so I don't have to look at them any longer.
Say no to wrong.
Learn to do good.

Work for justice.
Help the down-and-out.
Stand up for the homeless.
Go to bat for the defenseless."

– Isaiah 1:11-17, Message translation

"Here is a quick test to see if an idea is good. Do not ask if it feels good or has good intentions. Ask, 'Will it do good?' Will it make people kinder and more ethical? Will it encourage responsible behavior? Has it been tried before? And if so, what were the results?

"What matters is how you act. If you do something bad, it doesn't matter if you 'meant well.' If you do something good, it doesn't matter if you did it for 'selfish' reasons. So, spend much less time monitoring your motives, and far more time monitoring your actions." – Dennis Prager

"I have made this letter longer than usual, only because I have not had the time to make it shorter." – Blaise Pascal

Books by Brad Johnson:

Tomes Of A Healing Heart
Ignite Your Beacon: *Uncover Truth, Live With Intention, And Contribute Your Gifts To The World*
Writing Clout: *Make Money Online As A Writer Through Servant Leadership*
Lose Fat Rapidly: *8 Simple Steps To Drop Fat On A Vegan Diet*
133 Ways: *Boost Your Health, Slash Your Spending, Get Your Time Back and Revitalize Your Relationships*
Justice Is Served: *How And Why Christian Culture Inherently Supports Veganism*
365 Days Of Virtue *– Patience*
365 Days Of Virtue *– Excellence*
365 Days Of Virtue *– Leadership*
365 Days Of Virtue *– Ambition*

CreateSpace/Amazon Kindle
Justice Is Served:
How And Why Christian Culture Inherently Supports
Veganism
Brad Johnson

Published in the United States.

ISBN-13: 978-1540303998

ISBN-10: 1540303993

Printed by CreateSpace, a DBA of On-Demand Publishing, LLC

Asterisks throughout the book denote a relevant work or article cited at the end of the book.

About Brad Johnson

Brad Johnson is an entrepreneur whose creative bents have led him to merge the two interests whenever possible. He has cultivated a far-reaching range of experience within writing, editing, online content and publishing, and has lent his talents to a variety of online platforms, including Ezine Articles, Crowdsourcia, Vegaprocity and Constant Content.

Brad is the Top 15-selling Kindle author of *Lose Fat Rapidly: 8 Simple Steps To Drop Fat On A Vegan Diet*. He has also authored nine other books including *Ignite Your Beacon*, a self-development book that challenges the boundaries of messages typically found in self-help books. His Lifehack.org articles have been shared over 51,000 times, and his Quora posts have been viewed over 220,000 times.

A vegan of five years and counting, this lifestyle is a deep-seated conviction for Brad, and he is regularly learning, exploring and sharing more about this perspective. A musician of 17 years, Brad has performed across 14 different musical atmospheres throughout eight years of live playing, ranging from classical and orchestral to modern metal and hardcore. He is currently featured on or associated with 16 diverse recordings and is an active studio and live drummer.

Brad is a Certified Health and Nutrition Expert by <u>Primal Blueprint</u>, a Certified Life Coach by AUNLP and will obtain a Bachelor's of Health Sciences with an Emphasis in Health and Wellness in 2017.

Brad seeks to combine dreams with direction, ideas with execution and love with action. One of his grandest goals is to see that one day, all children throughout the world have access to the resources they need to realize their dreams, and can then make the world better because of it. Until then, he enjoys reading more books, dreaming up and executing projects and finding new ways to laugh at cats.

For free resources, book samples, useful information on writing and leadership or just to see what he's up to, visit Brad at BradleyJohnsonProductions.com

Table of Contents

Introduction

Before I lay out my most sincere and honest (not perfect) efforts of vegan apologetics for the Christian reader, I do want to state for the record (it may encourage you or change your perspective) that I have not been a vegan my whole life. Just like many of those who I reasonably assume to be reading this book – Christian or otherwise – I was born and raised on a diet that had a surplus of meat, cheese, dairy and eggs. I didn't give any of these foods a single critical thought until my late teenage years.

In writing this book, my effort is not to make you feel like a terrible person, to belittle your ambitions for a healthy life, to desecrate your familial traditions or ruthlessly offend you in any other deep way. No, my purpose in this book is to **tear down the unconditionally heartless and flagrantly depraved industry of animal consumption, and provide my best framework for a livable, prosperous and harmonious future for all creatures.**

Disclaimer: The people who will most readily identify with the messages of this book will be those who *identify on an emotional level with non-human animals.* It will be the people who are intrinsically motivated to bring about the world they see possible – not feeling coerced through guilt or mandated through various forces of conformity.

Also, this book will not have all the answers you need or want on veganism, but I will do my best to address the most important questions. Arguments to support a view are simply the icing on the cake; pure-hearted motivation and willing sacrifices that build a better world are the cake itself. In other words, you don't need to have every last answer in order to make a lifestyle change, but you do need a heart full of motivation and conviction that is ready to break out of a comfort zone.

Now with that out of the way, I can address a few other important matters. I understand that while this book is primarily written for Christian readers, the person currently holding a copy may not be a Christian. This is okay, and even awesome!

If you participate in a faith other than Christianity, I welcome your readership just as much as I do that of Christians. If you're secular or atheist (or anything else), the same concept applies! I'm happy for anyone to read this book, and I'm sure you'll be able to obtain insights from it. Whether you love or hate the book, please consider leaving a review on Amazon and sharing your thoughts. I seek honest reviews above anything else!

In order to get the most out of this book, I created a list of the book's core concepts below. These pillars of the book represent why this book is different from any other book on the subject, and a lens through which you can get the most out of the book:

CORE CONCEPTS

- Critical determinations between – and definitions *of* – wrong and right can be made
- We can build a comprehension of how to live

life off these definitions
- Cultural underpinnings must be examined and understood, for a right contemporary life to be lived
- Differences between wrong and right often have to do with justice
- It's the Christian's job to seek out the Christian definition of justice
- It's the Christian's job to uphold justice whenever possible
- Justice should inherently be a way of life
- Justice should be involved in as many choices as possible
- Justice should be all-inclusive, but place tangible emphasis on the least acknowledged members of society
- Justice is not a zero-sum game – It is, in fact, a positive-sum game
- Injustice reveals that oppressors must be obliterated and that the oppressed are not receiving justice
- Justice, from a holistic and truly centered worldview, necessitates veganism
- Christians are committed to drawing lines of justice when any situation calls for it
- The highest forms of human behavior permit plenty of space for logic, not simply emotional gratification or qualitative experiences
- It's up to us to maximize the true facets of our highest behavior

The Christian is called to imitate Christ in every facet of life. This includes **justice.**

So often throughout Christian life we're instructed to imitate godly Christians and to live the life Christ led, to the best of our ability. These are not bad recommendations; in fact, much good has come from them.

But in all our talk of Christian values, such as love, sacrifice, humility, stewardship, goodness, faithfulness, hope, patience and self-control, one characteristic that God esteems immensely is frequently overlooked. That characteristic is justice. Justice, in a nutshell, is this:

Consistently giving everyone what he or she deserves, with no partiality to the individual or group in question.

If we know non-human animals to be sentient and capable of suffering (which we do; more on this later), then a Christian's definition of justice *must include them*. Justice would be corrupt and self-serving if it did not encompass all who deserve justice.

Holistic, complete definitions of justice do not make excuses when facing traditions, habits, or pre-conceived notions. This is why justice, in some ways, must be an ever-evolving concept. Justice, especially Christian justice, necessitates a continual search for and openness to information that can heighten and deepen one's manifestations of justice.

Through this definition and the chapters within this book, we will explore why and how veganism is a natural extension of justice, especially within the Christian worldview. We will also acknowledge many of the common objections, observations and support made *by* Christians and *toward* Christians regarding veganism.

"A nation's greatness is measured by how it treats its weakest members." – Mahatma Ghandi

"'Speak up for the people who have no voice,
For the rights of all the down-and-outers.
Speak out for justice!
Stand up for the poor and destitute!'"

- Proverbs 31:8-9, MSG

Chapter 1: Why Do We (Still) Eat Meat?

"There are barbarians who seize this dog, who so prodigiously surpasses man in friendship, and nail him down to a table, and dissect him alive to show you the mezaraic veins. You discover in him all the same organs of feeling as in yourself. Answer me, Machinist, has Nature really arranged all the springs of feeling in this animal to the end that he might not feel? Has he nerves that he may be incapable of suffering?" – Voltaire

While the primary focus of this book is to make a watertight, impelling case for Christians worldwide to adopt a vegan diet, before the deepest contextual understanding of veganism can be reached, we must spend some time covering the basics of nutrition, health and the present state of non-human animal agriculture.

As shared in the core concepts section, critical determinations between – and definitions of – wrong and right can be made. In order for right living to be a pattern, we cannot leave moral actions – especially those regarding justice – in a state of limbo.

When facing an undesirable situation such as a political scandal or human rights fiasco, few people have difficulty deciding what should happen, or what should have happened. Yet, because we do not draw lines in the sand between what is objectively wrong and right, we can flounder in a gray zone of moral relativism. In other words, we rarely struggle to decide what is right in one specific scenario, but it is only when we objectively establish a right *against* a wrong that we can concretely observe and embody right action.

We can build a basis of how to live life off these definitions of wrong versus right. We can also help others create their idealized version of life and the world through our collective effort to identify, support and exist through communal justice and love.

We must be careful to allow all individuals plenty of freedom in their choices, however. In social psychology, we understand that the quickest way to create reactance and hostility in general is by removing freedom of choice. Despite my efforts to declare what is objectively wrong and right in the world through this book – and my effort to encourage such perspectives and actions in others – I fully recognize that many people will hate this book, either for what it declares or who is declaring it. Fortunately, that is ultimately none of my business. I am here to speak with Christians and non-Christians alike who are eager to bring about a holistically just world.

Cultural underpinnings must be examined and understood, for a right contemporary life to be lived. We no longer have the luxury of saying "I don't know" or "I didn't realize it was this bad." As it has been said countless times, "In the age of information, ignorance is a choice." And this couldn't be truer when it comes to non-human animal agriculture and veganism.

As of 2017, few people are born in strictly vegan households, which means you often have to go out of your way to learn about veganism in the first place. But in the same way that most forms of injustice are suppressed in order to prioritize profit for the oppressor, the needless violence against and bloodshed of non-human animals is concealed in order to perpetuate the unthinking preferences we have for our taste buds. And it is regarding such cultural traditions and taste bud preferences that we begin our examination of the truth behind non-human animal products.

The Non-Human Animal Product Myth

It has been ingrained into American ideology and culture for decades that humans need meat to survive. For that matter, it has been a societal indoctrination (within many cultures, not all) from the earliest stages of recorded history that it is okay to enslave and commodify animals.

The array of farm animals enjoying paradise on a lush, well-supplied ranch is the archetypal vision millions of Americans still superficially maintain. There's also the idea that if the non-human animal lived a wonderful life before it was slaughtered that the slaughter was somehow justified.

The assumption that meat is required in the human diet branches out of supposed nutritional merit. We're taught at a young age that non-human animal products provide a robust amount of protein for humans throughout all stages of life, and the media only reinforces this assertion. We then learn not to challenge the grounds of this claim via social pressure and social proof, allowing meat and dairy products to hold title as the kings of protein.

What's more, we conveniently ignore the surrounding factors of this ubiquitous protein glorification, as well as equally relevant questions. For example, within the Standard American Diet (SAD), 70 to 90 percent of all calories consumed are comprised of meat, dairy, eggs, added sugar, added fat and refined grains. We simply blindly consume these "meals" and food products without wondering if we may, in fact, be getting *too much* protein – let alone any other nutrient questions for the moment. It turns out that getting too much of anything, including protein, is a bad thing.*

We love to feel like we're getting the right type of protein in the right amounts when eating a diet inclusive of non-human animal products, but many of us neglect other macronutrients and micronutrients. No one walks around asking vegans where they get their fiber. At least, I've never been asked that, and I'm pretty sure dozens of other vegans can relate to this scenario. In fact, I've even had a meat-eating friend remark how much fiber my diet must provide!

All of this points to the fact that the vast majority of people are still confused and in the dark about nutrition. The greatest point of note here is a lot of it is not the typical person's fault. We live in a world where businesses, governments and corporations prioritize keeping people ill and uneducated rather than well and informed. Keeping people limited ensures they'll return to you for your "advice" or "expertise"; this in turn ensures profit over a long period of time. There's less profit to be had for doctors and hospitals in keeping people healthy.

Unfortunately, it's beyond the scope or intent of this book to dive deeply into the topic of overall healthcare and economic interactions with the vegan diet. To really drive this section home and provide information in a holistically accurate framework, however, we must briefly discuss the facts surrounding how well a vegan diet works.

Comparing Apples To Oranges

Humans are inclined to believe they know the best and most accurate information when their environment only reinforces their presuppositions. In other words, you may think that a few lights in your basement are really bright, and provide all the light you'll ever need. But you never really know the true meaning, extent, width and power of light until you experience sunlight.

Comparing the sun to a few string lights or lamps in your basement allows the truth to be seen in plain sight. Anything you thought you knew before – anything that seemed "infinitely true" – is now replaced by the larger, deeper, greater, truer understanding of more accurate information.

Now, this is not to utterly undermine everyone's presupposed notions about food, or to merely bully people. It is said to help you understand that, while you may not be incredibly far off in your current values, your daily behaviors and manifest practices may not be appropriately aligned yet. To put it another way, to decide if veganism feels right to you or not, you have to give it a good, square chance. Where many people begin (or get hung up) on veganism is how food tastes, and what they feel they're missing out on.

Plant-Based Flavor Power

Omnivores and meat lovers indulge in bragging about how tasty meat is, but when's the last time you experienced ribs without some kind of barbecue sauce, or even *a pasta dish* without some kind of marinara or alfredo sauce?

When vegetarians and vegans present others with alternatives to non-human animal products, omnivores regularly turn up their noses. It's strange to entertain this phenomenon in light of what non-human animal products *actually are*. The flesh of a non-human animal regularly contains veins, tendons, fat, sinew, blood vessels and, of course, the meat itself. When viewed in light of reality – especially with no flavors added – non-human animal products begin to lose their mainstream appeal.

What seems to be even more prevalent (and somewhat astounding) is that meat-eaters regularly think vegans won't be rigorous, persistent and logical in developing alternatives to meat products. Here's what I mean.

Looking back on the years I was a behavioral omnivore, I remember seeing vegetarian options on menus, and advertisements for various vegetarian and vegan products. The only prominent thought I remember hearing in my head was that I assumed vegetarian food might not be that filling. So I've always been a touch flabbergasted when meat-eaters discredit veg-heads as potentially having less exciting, mouthwatering food.

Think about it – when you're adding flavor to a portion of meat, how is that normally accomplished? Usually by adding an herb, spice or sauce of some kind. Sauces, herbs and spices typically always come from plant-based sources.

So, even the non-human animal products we enjoy are frequently, if not always, garnished and adorned with plants. Stews, soups, pasta dishes, rice dishes and fried or baked meals – some of the most common meals throughout the world – virtually always feature some kind of plant-based flavor upgrade.

(As a fun little experiment, next time you're making pasta, rice, polenta or some other grain-based dish, take a small portion out for yourself before the meal is complete. Then eat this by yourself. You'll notice how bland and "lifeless" the grain is, by comparison. This is why we always add spices, herbs, plant-based sauces and seasonings!)

Faux Meat

As countless passionate vegans have proclaimed, there has never been a better time in history to bountifully enjoy all the non-human animal product replacements that are available. Burgers, hot dogs, cheese, milk, pizzas, cookies, pies, brownies, fish and even *eggs* now **all** have vegan versions.

Most folks assume, without even giving these products a chance, that the taste and sensory experience will be inferior, simply because it's not what they are familiar with. And herein lies the truth: **people favor habit, convenience, taste and tradition above almost all else.** More on this later.

Even if we think about replacing our beloved non-human animal products with alternatives, we may feel overwhelmed, confused or simply in the dark about what alternatives work best. On my own path to veganism, I was unaware that almond milk even existed until I started looking up alternatives to dairy milk. The vegan food industry still has fewer marketing dollars than their competitors, but this obstacle will eventually be overcome (if need be). Furthermore, it all comes down to supply and demand.

In so many cases, people purchase food products that they are familiar with simply because they're not as aware of other options. Meat, cheese, milk and eggs are so ubiquitous because they're marketed so heavily, and so deeply culturally ingrained. Your subconscious mind is going to more easily recall (and further reinforce) what your conscious thoughts and senses are most often greeted with.

In addition to these factors, virtually all non-human animal products are heavily subsidized. The United States government in particular is a convenient example of this. Meat and dairy lobbyists are some of the most successful of their kind, because they take a chunk of their profits and further encourage U.S. citizens to gobble down their products like there's no tomorrow.

LearnVest, a financial education company, ran a study on non-human animal product cost myths in 2010.* Their study revealed that vegan diets are cheaper on average by $3.50 per day, all other factors held equal of course. I.E., you could purchase less or more food than is outlined in their infographic, but the costs would proportionally still be the same.

Occasionally, we or someone we know will discover they have dietary restrictions. This typically puts a whole new spin on how people approach handling their diet. When a "want" or "could" is pushed to a "need" or "must", the human mind is able to conceive and achieve far more effectively. It stands as openly confusing, then, that people think they have no power to change their habits before a stronger necessity influences what they conceive as genuinely possible. When we are faced with a greater pain if our habits don't change, it becomes far simpler for our emotions and thoughts to create a pathway that acknowledges effective, long-term solutions.

What's The Deal With Veganism, And Is It Really Optimal?

For the idea that humans require meat in the diet to be true, we would have to see example after example of poor health and swifter death when meat is removed from consumption. Instead, we see the exact opposite. There are reams of studies that point to how less meat and non-human animal products in general only improve one's health and drastically reduce the chances of abysmal health drawbacks.

In 2009, the American Dietetic Association (ADA) released a study stating that properly planned vegetarian and vegan diets are able to provide all necessary macro- and micronutrients, and are healthy and suitable for all stages and forms of human life.* Another popular individual in vegan spheres, registered dietician Jack Norris, openly shares vegan nutritional information, especially high-level studies released by nutritional and medical journals. Norris' websites can be found at JackNorrisRD.com and VeganHealth.org. *The Proceedings of the Nutritional Society* also released a study in 2006, stating that vegetarian and vegan diets are abundant in beneficial, nutrient-dense foods, and that health drawbacks are, in essentially all ways, absent.
It is worth mentioning here that by no means am I saying you will become immune or "perfect" if/when you become vegan. It is simply to illustrate that vegan diets have been examined by top-shelf scientists and nutritionists, and found to be completely valid and void of nearly all chronic disease agents.

The consumption of meat – a non-human animal's flesh – is hardly ever spoken about as nutritionally sound in all contexts. In her book, *Why We Love Dogs, Eat Pigs and Wear Cows,* Melanie Joy helped clarify the reality that we even have different terms for commercial meat and non-human animal products. Rather than calling it cow meat, we call it beef, or a burger. Instead of mentioning our breakfast with pig flesh, we rave about the bacon we had. Instead of calling it a duck liver, we revel in the "sophistication" that comes with talking about foie gras.

Rare are the times indeed when anyone takes a moment to consider how that meat got from the farm to their plate (Joy's book is highly recommended for further reading on this topic). When thinking about all of the steps between a live, usually sick non-human animal and a slab of meat on the plate, few people immediately recognize how complex, emotionally taxing and gruesome a process it is.

Even hearing or seeing a condensed version of a slaughterhouse procedure is enough to make most folks reconsider the meaning of eating (or commodifying) non-human animals at all.

According to the science and studies that are presently available, there is no conceivable way humans have needed to consume meat. The only semi-understandable scenario here is if/when small tribes of travelers decided to kill a non-human animal and eat it to survive in desolate environmental conditions.

Our bodies are not equipped with the raw tools and features required to capture other animals and eat them in the wild. Rather, our bodily shapes, features and functions are all geared towards frugivorous herbivorism, or a fruit- and vegetable-based diet.

Our teeth sizes and shapes are extremely similar to that of plant-eating creatures. We have thinner, flatter teeth in front to help crunch and chomp into plant matter, and molars and grinding teeth in back to mash food up more effectively, creating a bolus to swallow. Our jaws move side to side rather than strictly vertically, indicating our mouths and jaws are designed for breaking down rough plant matter, not raw meat that must be consumed quickly.

Our digestive tracts are lengthier than that of carnivorous creatures, which enables our bodies to pull more nutrients out of our food over a longer period of time. The food we eat (or are designed to optimally consume) is highly fibrous, requiring more digestive time in the first place. Carnivorous animals, such as the cheetah or lion, have shorter digestive tracts that have higher amounts of hydrochloric acid in them. This chemical is what allows these creatures to digest the meat of other animals in a quick and efficient manner. Human stomachs have *a fraction* of the hydrochloric acid of carnivore stomachs, because our entire diet is designed to have no need to digest foods at such an acidic capacity.

Before we go any further, you may be thinking: "Wait a second, Brad. You're talking about how humans shouldn't be eating meat, but you're providing examples of animals that *do* consume meat? What gives?!"

This is a fair question. But the answer is, the matter of what lions, cheetahs and other obligate carnivores eat is none of our business as humans. That is to say what lions do or do not eat is of no dietary concern for us, because we as humans are drastically different creatures. These reasons are precisely why I provided the examples above. Apples should not be compared to oranges, just like non-human animal diets should not be compared to human diets.

There is also the fact that obligate carnivores, as far as we know, are not consciously choosing their food sources every day. If they were, we would probably see different behaviors and food gathering practices in addition to bodily adaptations. But science points in a different direction, showing that non-human animals have fewer cognitive capabilities and freedoms than we do, and that the livelihood and wellbeing of these creatures is far more dependent upon our choices than we realize.

Natural Carnivorous Instincts

Take a moment to recount your morning today. After waking up, perhaps you went to the bathroom, changed clothes or something of the like. You may have consumed a glass of water.

Now, if you're the type of person who typically eats breakfast, what did you have this morning? You may have poured yourself a bowl of cereal, but you also may have cracked open an egg and fried some bacon. But, why did you do all of that? Why did you make that particular choice? In other words, why didn't you step outside to your backyard for a nice, juicy squirrel you could pounce on, skin and fry up in the pan?

At first glance, this scenario is laughable and seems so

absurd. The truth is, *it is* absurd! There's no reason at all for a human to have to walk outside upon waking up, prepare weapons to kill a squirrel, and then do so to feed oneself for breakfast.

Yet, no one bats an eye or gives it a second thought when they see an omelet being made from a hen's menstrual cycle or a few strips of pig flesh being prepared in a skillet. These actions and choices for food have been culturally ingrained in us for decades, even centuries, and most people aren't interested in questioning why these things happen or challenging the status quo.

There are four main reasons people eat non-human animal products day after day, year after year:

Habit: "I've always had lunch like this; what's the need to change it?"

Convenience: "It's so easy to stay where I'm at right now and keep eating this way. Adopting new choices or looking for alternatives is too much work."

Taste: "I just absolutely love how meat and non-human animal products taste. How would I get on without them?"

Tradition: "It's what my family has always done. They'd probably be offended if I tried a vegan diet for too long."

Perhaps in reading these, you've found you resonate with one or even all of them. And to be honest, it's completely understandable. I was once there as well.

When I was younger, perhaps in late grade school or junior high, I would hear talk of vegetarians and people who abstained from meat in their diet. For the most part, when I was thinking about it at all, I thought it was cool and definitely respected these individuals for their choices in life, but I knew very little about it beyond this, and certainly didn't think I would ever walk this path myself.

As I got older, I met more vegetarians and saw a little bit more about this lifestyle in the media. As I would continue on, consuming the foods I found so enjoyable and tasty, I would wonder how these vegetarians "made it work." Were they so content with brightly colored vegetables and fruits all day? Was this all it took to maintain a proper diet and still enjoy all your food every time you sat down to a meal?

Like nearly every other person, I wondered how these vegetarians got their protein. What took me years to discover – and then challenge – was the fact that across the world and particularly in the United States, it's ingrained and embedded in us that it's essential to get protein from non-human animal sources – that any other food source is inferior or irrelevant. The majority of Americans still believe this, due to the lobbyists and media forces that have defended non-human animal products and sought to stigmatize many other nutritional truths.

We've seen it for years: children walk around in schools where posters, textbooks and other forms of media tout the benefits of milk, cheese and various non-human animal products. We're taught from a young age that non-human animal products have a well-earned place on everyone's plate, and to critique

34

them as unnecessary or even detrimental is an awkward and occasionally incendiary social sin.

This was particularly popular and relevant during the "Got Milk?" poster series. This was an uncommonly intriguing case, because what ended up as a multi-decade cultural phenomenon began as a slightly gimmicky question scribbled on a boardroom whiteboard.*

We were taught to love milk, to appreciate it, to celebrate it, to have desserts with it and to go out and purchase more whenever we ran out. "Got Milk?" became more popular than any other commercial beverage phrase,* and – just like countless other cultural trends – when something has been around long enough, people rarely question it.

Unfortunately, "taught" doesn't always mean something is correct. As we journey through adult life, we must constantly be challenging our "maps," as M. Scott Peck (author of *The Road Less Traveled*) would say. For example, a young white boy may be "taught" at an early age that he's not supposed to spend time with African American young boys, because it's simply what Mommy and Daddy said.

His parents may not give him further reasoning at the time for whatever reason, but as this young boy grows up, he must realize that his parents have (heinously) misled him – that they've initiated a path of racism – and he must rely on himself, friends and other trusted figures to reprogram his mind *out of* racism.

This same framework applies to non-human animals. Many of us have been indoctrinated from our earliest years of cognition that eating non-human animals and animal products is not only acceptable and normal, but highly nutritious and encouraged virtually everywhere.

For example, when taking the family out to a posh dinner or traveling abroad, it's commonplace to see quite a bit of money being spent on meals that focus on non-human animal products. Grilled chicken flesh, baby cow meat and sea creatures are all common dinner selections at higher-end restaurants. And typically, no one bats an eye or squirms in their seat.

It all has to do with familiarity. Professor Stanley Milgram discovered through his experiments in the 1960s that most people are willing to obey authority figures and social pressure, even when the experimenter's requests conflict with the subject's conscience. If we peel back a few layers of the world we face today, we see there's no difference.

Hundreds of thousands of kids throughout the United States alone have grown up eating many or all of the following: chicken nuggets, hot dogs, nachos, mac and cheese, Bosco sticks, pizza, chocolate milk and desserts of every imaginable kind. All of these have some kind of non-human animal product in them. The most common is cheese – which contains casomorphin, the enzyme in dairy products that is actually addictive.

Parents and grandparents are all too familiar with these "foods" as well – both because their children eat them and because they have consumed these products. Non-human animal-product-centric meals have been around for thousands of years; they have simply taken different forms as cultures and societies have experienced progress and changes.

In truth, you are not immediately at fault for raising your eyebrow or grimacing when seeing a vegetarian or vegan option on a menu. As humans, we're already wired to regard the strange and unfamiliar as bizarre, at the very least. Living a life surrounded by people, experiences, thoughts and actions that are familiar feels good, and no one is really to blame for that.

The catch is that entire industries, businesses and marketers have become so slick over recent decades to such a degree that we more often question outliers than we do our own presupposed morals and value-oriented notions. In other words, we live in such a sterile world where hundreds of choices are rammed down our throat daily, making us more prone to consider black sheep irrelevant than to actually examine why the black sheep exists and what it is doing.

It does take effort to go against the grain – especially if you come to consider going *with* the grain an immoral route. Onlookers will examine your new course of action, compare it with their own and react based on how your actions make them feel.

This is not necessarily a bad thing, but when you take a stand against social and cultural norms, be prepared to be met first with ignorance and later resistance.

Non-Human Animal Abuse

It can be all too easy to think three thoughts about animal abuse:

1- We may think animal abuse is limited to acts such as those Michael Vick and his chums committed, where an individual and their actions are blasted to mega proportions in the media. This is often all most people think of non-human animal abuse on a given day.

2- We may think non-human animal abuse now being considered a felony in the United States is a joke and a waste of criminal justice leverage.

3- We may think it is okay to treat some non-human animals well while others suffer incalculable pain and die at the hands of our un-scrutinized preferences.

None of these mindsets are okay, and each can be brought into the true light with monumental facts and sound logic.

A) First, the Michael Vick scenario. Vick was a widely celebrated NFL star, being the second-highest-paid sports professional at one point. Sadly, his public reputation (and a good chunk of his professional career) took a turn for the worse in 2007 when he was indicted for dogfighting charges with three other individuals.

Vick's story does two bad things. **It brings a lot of attention to Michael Vick and how what he did was a terrible thing.** Honestly, yes, what he did *was* a terrible thing. But it's the media's classic move to aggrandize a "villain" and push out this image and mantra of fear into the public. Fundamentally, it is used as an effort to make people only view someone's bad side, as though there's no bias taking place through the media's coverage whatsoever.

We see this with school shootings where the perpetrator's negative image is used in the likeness of Batman's Joker, where one must simply fear the villain at all costs, thereby removing the human element, as well as taking the limelight off the victim(s), which is where the majority of attention should fall anyways. This relationship increases in significance the more vulnerable the victim(s) is/are.

B) Second, considering it a joke to label non-human animal abuse as felonies is not a waste of time. It is now a well-documented fact that dozens of serial killers began by abusing non-human animals first, and that violent individuals in general often practice with innocent non-human creatures.

Through this fact alone we can see that protecting non-human animals not only protects them, it's a safeguard for human lives and against all forms of violence. Destruction and violence anywhere should be subject to rigorous examination and a caution on the side of prevention.

C) Third, arbitrary cultural lines between acceptable non-human animal violence and unacceptable bloodshed are exactly that – arbitrary. Humans are not necessarily to blame for *all* of this – at least until a point. A massive part of the human experience is living life and making choices in social circles, many of which interact with cultural traditions and pastimes.

When it comes to food, countless cultural backgrounds involve dishes that incorporate some type of non-human animal product. Non-human animals have been commodified for so long under the hand of human authority and oppression that we hardly question it anymore.

As a child, I certainly did not question how tasty chocolate milkshakes were, or how aromatic a burger may be, along with dozens of other non-human animal-centric foods. I do admit these foods taste great – but only within the framework of other non-human animal-based foods. Genuine taste in its own right cannot possibly be made valid in light of immeasurable suffering of innocent lives.

Ralph Waldo Emerson captured this observation accurately in one of his musings about slaughterhouses and the animal agriculture industry:

"You have just dined, and however scrupulously the slaughterhouse is concealed in the graceful distance of miles, there is complicity."

Humans Are Born Vegan

We rarely take time to think about it, but humans are born vegan. I would go so far as to say that even our instincts are vegan, but this is a redundant statement – in a beneficial way.

Consider an infant, only a few months old, who is playing around in his or her crib. Now imagine the infant is given both an apple and a rabbit. Would the baby kill and eat the rabbit and play with the apple?

Or would it play with the rabbit and eat the apple?

This thought may have brought a smile to your lips, and understandably so. We typically only consider the consequences of circumstances we are faced with in the present moment, or those that may immediately threaten ourselves or our loved ones.

However, when we take the time to examine our daily lifestyle choices up close to see if they fit our ideals of a good and just world, there is a high likelihood we will be greeted by less-than-comforting thoughts. Often – if not always – the quest towards goodness and justice requires resistance against "normal" ways of life and typical frames of mind.

We've now covered some of the raw essentials surrounding why a vegan diet works and is even optimal. We've also covered a few core misconceptions about non-human animal cruelty. For further reading, I suggest looking at the recommendations at the end of this book. Next, let's dive into the intro of this book's core message: how and why Christian culture inherently values veganism, and how and why Christians can benefit themselves and others by adhering to an identity-level vegan lifestyle.

Christians Must Lead Via Christ's Example

When we begin with the goal of emulating Christ at all possible opportunities, and fixate our minds on humility in all avenues, the windows of abundant change open up like never before. Christ embodied dozens of characteristics that can literally alter the face of interaction we have with others, and ourselves, if we are but mindful long enough to take action on them.

For those who have been vegetarian or vegan for any length of time, it is all too common to be asked why one has chosen this path, or to even be complimented in the manner of, "You're such a good person!/I could never do that!" It is even easier to smile and perhaps blush at such words, but it takes revolutionary-caliber courage to acknowledge the compliment and pass the credit along to another source. In this case, moving the credit of one's actions towards Christ is a pinnacle choice. After all, when we are removing non-human animal products from our diet in favor of other sources of nutrients (and for reasons *beyond* personal health), isn't this a raw embodiment of some of Christ's core values? Sacrifice, humility, compassion, courage and honesty are legitimate efforts to strive after and encourage in others.

The World Notices Genuine Christians

Far be it from me to say that Christians are perfect people, or that we've got our act completely together. In fact, it's the opposite. Christians are imperfect like anyone else, and we have a long way to go before we can say Christianity is on a united front.

Despite this (and whether you are a Christian reader or otherwise), the world does pay attention to individuals who actually practice what they preach. This extends outside Christianity too. If you're someone who talks about virtue and justice, and you walk it every day (despite however muddled another individual's concept of justice may be), you are a living, breathing example of love and truth.

Within the claims and goals Christians profess, we have a responsibility to uphold said goals via our actions. If we really want to make this world better, it requires teamwork on a massive scale – **a scale so inclusive it's never been seen before.**

Recognizing the fact that over seven billion humans share the Earth, understanding we have to learn how to work with each other is no longer a debate. **It's a bare-minimum *necessity.*** What *is* in question is how we can more efficiently reach universally beneficial solutions.

Ever since the dawn of the religion, Christians have received negative attention and been forced to cope with those opposing their message. The very figure who the religion is based off of, Jesus Christ, is likely the most polarizing figure in all of history. Individuals were either all-in and completely devoted to discipleship, or were the very names and faces seeking His demise.

Regardless of where you stand on Christianity, bringing a vegan world to pass – for the benefit of all – will take collaboration with those you haven't met or worked with before. It may even require working with people you otherwise "hate."

Chapter 1 Thesis:

Non-human animal products are not essential for human consumption and health. They also perpetuate direct damage upon multiple resources/causes many humans care about, such as environmental protection, human rights, non-human animal liberation and global peace. Christians must be committed to justice through veganism in order to properly and holistically live out Christian values.

"In their behavior towards creatures, all men were Nazis. The smugness with which man could do with other species as he pleased exemplified the most extreme racist theories, the principle that might is right."
– Isaac Bashevis Singer

Chapter 2: What The Bible Says About Consuming Non-Human Animals As Food

"The assumption that animals are without rights, and the illusion that our treatment of them has no moral significance, is a positively outrageous example of Western crudity and barbarity. Universal compassion is the only guarantee of morality." – Arthur Schopenhauer, German philosopher

Ever since Christianity began, people have been eating meat. But people were eating meat before Christianity came into existence, as well.

People have also abstained from meat consumption before Christianity, and clearly, this lifestyle hasn't disappeared at all. There are diehard meat fans and there are diehard vegans.

What seems all too common to witness, however, is a particular combination of a few characteristics. Bible-believing, often politically conservative Christians represent a large chunk of the United States' frequent red meat consumers.* Groupthink appears to be afoot, because it seems every self-respecting conservative Christian be a non-human animal product consumer. It's been the *tradition* for so long that few people take the time or effort to question it.

The first truth about meat eating for Christians can be found in chapter one of Genesis. Genesis 1:28-31 patently states God's original design for human food, and it's a vegan blueprint.

"God blessed them:
     'Prosper! Reproduce! Fill Earth! Take charge!
  Be responsible for fish in the sea and birds in the air,
     for every living thing that moves on the face of Earth.'
29-30 Then God said, 'I've given you
     every sort of seed-bearing plant on Earth
  And every kind of fruit-bearing tree,
     given them to you for food.
  To all animals and all birds,
     everything that moves and breathes,

I give whatever grows out of the ground for food.'
   And there it was.
31 God looked over everything he had made;
   it was so good, so very good!
It was evening, it was morning—
Day Six."

Within the first chapter of Genesis, we see God explicitly state His desired plan for our diet. What is particularly noteworthy is that God points out the variety of foods we get to take part in. He states that "every sort" of seed-bearing plant and fruit-bearing tree is ours to consume, and share with our fellow humans. Last time I checked, "every sort" of fruit and plant includes thousands of varieties and styles, of which any individual would never tire – provided variety in cooking and flavors are available.

For those who have recently transitioned to veganism or are considering the switch, it can certainly appear challenging to consider what you might eat. However, when we take a step back, it's much easier to see that – as behavioral omnivores – we compare a few dozen routine non-human animal products (cows, pigs, chickens, lambs, fish) to the hundreds and thousands of vegan products that are available.

It's completely understandable to feel apprehensive about how to replace dearly held, familiar meals with new vegan options. The average consumer has grown used to some form of meat or cheese product in nearly every meal – and not by their own volition all the time. Non-human animal products are routinely marketed to all ages, genders and ethnicities for breakfast, lunch, dinner, snacks and dessert.

According to Dr. Michael Greger, creator and operator of NutritionFacts.org, the average American household rotates through seven to 10 dinners per month. This means that, at least from a starting point, you'd only need to find this many meals to replace or veganize in order to eat vegan every night. Then, you can easily move the same behavior to your lunches and breakfasts, and you'll have a fully vegan month prepared in no time.

A Christian Perspective On The "Garden Of Vegan"

The situation all Christians are faced with is that of God's sovereignty and omniscience. If God's original design for Eden (and therefore all of humanity and creation) was vegan, who are we to try to distort, mangle and desecrate that?

We don't know for sure if all non-human animals in Eden were fully vegan before the Fall. But the overwhelmingly vast majority of this conversation is presently irrelevant, because there's abundant evidence that humans cause everything that is wrong with this planet.* If humans disappeared, all other life on this planet would flourish.*

Our family and ancestors are only partially to blame. It's one thing to be brought up in a family where non-human animal consumption is routine and unquestioned. And let's be honest, this is most families.*

It's another ordeal entirely to become aware of completely relevant truths, absorb the current state of affairs with our world and continue on one's way as though nothing has been presented to you. We cannot expect to be all that Christ has called us to be (let alone what the world genuinely expects of Christians) if we witness ugly truth and turn our backs due to discomfort.

Did white Christians who knew the truth stand and watch as other whites perpetuated violence against blacks? Did justice-seeking blacks let their white friends stand idly by during years of continued segregation? Did women seeking suffrage allow unambitious, unconvinced women to mope around? Do members of the LGBTQ community refuse to set up safe gathering areas and avoid talking about their own lifestyles?

We have a duty to share the truth we know with those who claim to be on our side but take no clear actions based on that truth. Freedom is always a battle.

God states in Genesis 1:28 that humans are charged with *dominion* over all non-human animals. Dominion can mean a multitude of realities depending on whom you ask, but in this context, there's only one sensible answer. Dominion most closely means **sovereignty over something or someone else.** Humans have therefore been charged with protecting the life, freedom and happiness of all other creatures on Earth.

The editors of the Life Application Study Bible (of Tyndale House Publishers) also share the following thoughts in their footnotes for Genesis 1:28:

"When God delegated some of His authority to the human race, he expected us to take responsibility for the environment and the other creatures that share our planet. We must not be careless and wasteful as we fulfill this charge. God was careful how He made this Earth; we must not be careless about how we take care of it."

I'm not implying or stating the editors of Life Application Study Bible are vegans. However, for those who legitimately contemplate the logic of taking the best care of the Earth possible and studying the facts available,* what other choice are we left with? The optimal way to care for God's creation, non-human animals and ourselves is to go vegan.

Doesn't The Bible Allow – Or Even Encourage – Consumption Of Animals? (And Other Common Christian-Based Arguments Against Veganism)

Genesis 9:1-4

[1-4] "God blessed Noah and his sons: He said, 'Prosper! Reproduce! Fill the Earth! Every living creature—birds, animals, fish—will fall under your spell and be afraid of you. You're responsible for them. All living creatures are yours for food; just as I gave you the plants, now I give you everything else. Except for meat with its lifeblood still in it—don't eat that.'"

What we witness here is God stating that non-human animals are acceptable as sources of food for humans. This discussion took place after the Fall, as well as immediately following the Flood. We must closely examine the permissions God is giving to Noah and his family in order to reach an appropriate conclusion.

First of all, stepping out of the Ark right after a flood means the Earth was essentially barren. Sure, some plant life was already starting to grow again, but Noah and his family would have had extremely little to rely on for food, even including any food left over in their boat.

God understood that they would likely go hungry for weeks or even months at a time if they had no immediate food sources. So, while it is preferable for zero non-human animals to be consumed, God provided choice – the freedom to consume something other than plants for food within a set context.

In other words, this freedom God allowed is not a free license to simply eat whatever we want, whenever we want. This background knowledge must be taken in context, and the logic within the story must be applied to contemporary scenarios that 99 percent of us experience daily.

This segment of Genesis 9 can be appropriately coupled with the common "deserted island" argument many vegetarians and vegans receive from omnivores and meat-lovers. The argument generally goes like this:

"I understand you prefer not to eat meat and everything, but what if you were stranded on a deserted island for weeks at a time? Would you eat meat then?"

The reason many people offer up this argument is because they're looking for a situation in which a veg-head would be cornered and have *no other choice* but to consume a non-human animal. This argument can be logically critiqued from at least two standpoints: what I call the "solitude" counterargument and the "abundance" counterargument.

Solitude

First, few people realize the implication they're making when they say "deserted island." Sure, the presupposed scenario is that there are no other humans on the island, but if we really take this statement to task, "deserted" authentically means *no other form of sentient life.*

We've already covered elsewhere in the book how non-human animals are sentient creatures deserving of a free life, so in this hypothetical scenario, all that's left on the island would be plant life, organic matter, and one human. By default, this already illuminates the fact there would be no non-human animals to eat, even if given the choice. It's through this lens we can recognize that a deserted island really means solitude.

Abundance

Second, as I mentioned before, people who offer up this argument really aren't putting their own logic to task in the first place. They're simply looking to fabricate an isolated example of when a veg-head would "cave" and consume a non-human animal. Yet, simple common sense shows us how incredibly rare it would be to find anyone completely isolated on a deserted island these days. In his book *Meat Logic*, Charles Horn refers to this type of argument as a lose-lose scenario.

The vast majority of travel (including all airplanes,

boats, trains, buses and cars) is incredibly efficient and safe these days, and I cannot say I've ever encountered a single friend or family member who was isolated on an island for any length of time. I've heard of flight delays and terrible traffic, yes, but even within these instances, no one is further than 10 to 15 minutes away from a food kiosk, restaurant or grocery store.

Meat eaters try to construct an illogical and, frankly, completely unlikely scenario for vegans to get them to fold while ignoring the **free, abundant choices that are consistently available to them in normal, everyday life.** In other words, behavioral omnivores attempt to pressure vegans into hypothetically consuming meat while neglecting their own responsibility – and completely available freedom – to eat what's beneficial for themselves, non-human animals and the Earth.

Let's also keep in mind...

Remember, Genesis 1:29 is where God lays out the original plan for Eden, which was vegan. Before humanity became sinful, we had no urge, desire or interest in consuming non-human animals for food.

Romans 14 – "The Weak and the Strong"

"Accept the one whose faith is weak, without quarreling over disputable matters. ² One person's faith allows them to eat anything, but another, whose faith is weak, eats only vegetables. ³ The one who eats everything must not treat with contempt the one who does not, and the one who does not eat everything must not judge the one who does, for God has accepted them. **4** Who are you to judge someone else's servant? To their own master, servants stand or fall. And they will stand, for the Lord is able to make them stand.

5 "One person considers one day more sacred than another; another considers every day alike. Each of them should be fully convinced in their own mind. **6** Whoever regards one day as special does so to the Lord. Whoever eats meat does so to the Lord, for they give thanks to God; and whoever abstains does so to the Lord and gives thanks to God. **7** For none of us lives for ourselves alone, and none of us dies for ourselves alone. **8** If we live, we live for the Lord; and if we die, we die for the Lord. So, whether we live or die, we belong to the Lord. **9** For this very reason, Christ died and returned to life so that he might be the Lord of both the dead and the living.

10 "You, then, why do you judge your brother or sister? Or why do you treat them with contempt? For we will all stand before God's judgment seat. **11** It is written:
"'As surely as I live,' says the Lord,
'every knee will bow before me;
     every tongue will acknowledge God.'"
12 So then, each of us will give an account of ourselves to God.

13 "Therefore let us stop passing judgment on one another. Instead, make up your mind not to put any stumbling block or obstacle in the way of a brother or sister. **14** I am convinced, being fully persuaded in the Lord Jesus, that nothing is unclean in itself. But if anyone regards something as unclean, then for that person it is unclean.

[15] "If your brother or sister is distressed because of what you eat, you are no longer acting in love. Do not by your eating destroy someone for whom Christ died. [16] Therefore do not let what you know is good be spoken of as evil. [17] For the kingdom of God is not a matter of eating and drinking, but of righteousness, peace and joy in the Holy Spirit, [18] because anyone who serves Christ in this way is pleasing to God and receives human approval.

[19] *"Let us therefore make every effort to do what leads to peace and to mutual edification. [20] Do not destroy the work of God for the sake of food.* All food is clean, but it is wrong for a person to eat anything that causes someone else to stumble. [21] *It is better not to eat meat or drink wine or to do anything else that will cause your brother or sister to fall.*

[22] "So whatever you believe about these things keep between yourself and God. Blessed is the one who does not condemn himself by what he approves. [23] But whoever has doubts is condemned if they eat, because their eating is not from faith; and everything that does not come from faith is sin.

(All emphases mine, NIV translation)

Each sentence throughout Romans 14 is to be taken on an individual basis. The entire chapter is partly literal, partly not. The concept here is not that people are literally *weak,* physically or mentally, if they're vegetarians or vegans. The idea is the following:

"We should not change our *own* lifestyle simply to accommodate *another's* lifestyle **unless it is causing harm.**"

Now, does this passage mean we should only and always assess our lifestyle choices based on the direct effects towards those we call friends, family and loved ones? Not necessarily. I'll use my own background as an example.

I was born and raised in the Midwestern United States to an upper-middle class family that had most of the same habits as other families within our demographic. We attended sports events, enjoyed fancier meals from time to time, shared traditional meals and many other events involving specific food choices. I was grateful for the experiences at the time and I thought nothing of my family's choices, especially because we were doing what others did.

Until I was 18, I had never really questioned what any type of food choice was about. I loved candy and chocolate chip cookies (as many young boys do) and still knew I couldn't have them all the time, but I didn't care much about anything else. I still remember my high school dietary habits: gorging on bagels with cream cheese, pasta salad, ham and cheese sandwiches and massive chocolate chip cookies, all of which I now cringe in horror at.

When I had graduated from high school and went off to my first year of college, I began reading and learning more about dietary differences, the effects of non-human animal products on human health, chronic diseases and what the average human could do about all of them. I quickly learned that all chronic diseases and ailments – at least the ones that plague dozens of developed countries – can be thwarted or reversed through simple dietary changes. As I read more articles online and watched videos, I decided I couldn't blindly consume the same foods over and over again and risk future health woes.

It was shortly after turning 19 that I stopped eating most meat. Not long after that I stopped eating seafood, and it was the next year that I went vegan. Now, let's incorporate that summary with where I'm at presently, as well as how I've interacted with friends and family during my transitions.

In our "concrete," tangible, daily lives, we rarely if ever witness how non-human animals are bred, confined and slaughtered for our food preferences. It's for this very reason that Melanie Joy's book holds so much weight. Humans are emotional creatures who respond best to concrete or tangible evidence of things, because "true-to-life" evidence of anything makes it easier to adjust one's thinking and behavior around a subject.

Through learning about the torture and death we inflict on non-human animals, I unmistakably saw how my former diet was causing harm. I could no longer (in good conscience) continue consuming non-human animal products – for my health, that of the Earth, as a Christian and as an example for others.

Acts 10:1-23 – Peter's Vision

Cornelius Calls for Peter

"At Caesarea there was a man named Cornelius, a centurion in what was known as the Italian Regiment. ² He and all his family were devout and God-fearing; he gave generously to those in need and prayed to God regularly. ³ One day at about three in the afternoon he had a vision. He distinctly saw an angel of God, who came to him and said, 'Cornelius!'

⁴ "Cornelius stared at him in fear. 'What is it, Lord?' he asked.
The angel answered, 'Your prayers and gifts to the poor have come up as a memorial offering before God. ⁵ Now send men to Joppa to bring back a man named Simon who is called Peter. ⁶ He is staying with Simon the tanner, whose house is by the sea.'

⁷ "When the angel who spoke to him had gone, Cornelius called two of his servants and a devout soldier who was one of his attendants. ⁸ He told them everything that had happened and sent them to Joppa.

Peter's Vision

⁹ "About noon the following day as they were on their journey and approaching the city, Peter went up on the roof to pray. ¹⁰ He became hungry and wanted something to eat, and while the meal was being prepared, he fell into a trance.¹¹ He saw heaven opened and something like a large sheet being let down to earth by its four corners. ¹² It contained all kinds of four-footed animals, as well as reptiles and birds. ¹³ Then a voice told him, 'Get up, Peter. Kill and eat.'

¹⁴ "'Surely not, Lord!' Peter replied. 'I have never eaten anything impure or unclean.'
¹⁵ The voice spoke to him a second time, 'Do not call anything impure that God has made clean.'

16 This happened three times, and immediately the sheet was taken back to heaven.

17 While Peter was wondering about the meaning of the vision, the men sent by Cornelius found out where Simon's house was and stopped at the gate. **18** They called out, asking if Simon who was known as Peter was staying there.

19 While Peter was still thinking about the vision, the Spirit said to him, 'Simon, three men are looking for you. **20** So get up and go downstairs. Do not hesitate to go with them, for I have sent them.'

21 "Peter went down and said to the men, 'I'm the one you're looking for. Why have you come?'

22 The men replied, "We have come from Cornelius the centurion. He is a righteous and God-fearing man, who is respected by all the Jewish people. A holy angel told him to ask you to come to his house so that he could hear what you have to say."**23** Then Peter invited the men into the house to be his guests.

(NIV translation)

A lot of Christian behavioral omnivores like to use this passage as a way to "thwart" Christian vegetarians or vegans, but the story runs significantly deeper than the surface meaning. When reading in context, we understand this section cannot be taken literally. If you look into the context of Acts 10 and what was happening in those verses, this passage is about Jews and Gentiles, not about non-human animals versus veganism.

Wasn't Meat Consumption Accepted And Even Encouraged In Bible Times?

Every human I know who's of a sound mind is against unnecessary non-human animal abuse. And I've met *a lot* of sound-minded humans. And yet every day, three times a day, most of us consume dead non-human animals for food. *Completely unnecessarily.*

As mentioned throughout this book, the American Dietetic Association (ADA) declared in 2009 that a properly planned vegan diet is completely healthy and nutritious for all stages and forms of human life. The ADA would have to be lying for non-human animal products to be necessary or beneficial, nutritionally speaking. Yes, the Great Fall and flood changed the landscape of food (contextually and temporarily), but that doesn't excuse anyone from doing good when and where they can.

Saying we can enslave and exploit non-human animals for our pleasure because the Fall broke our relationship with them is unthinkable, because by that logic we can excuse sinful behavior towards all sentient creatures, including humans. Being weighed down by sin while on the Earth is no excuse not to strive for good. Death is needed to pay for sin, but non-human animal death was never required. God actually directly talks about this in Isaiah, Jeremiah, Micah and a few other books.

Non-human animal sacrifice in Bible times was a pleasure-driven action from humans; never something requested or ultimately required by God. What's more, God makes it clear that the blood of a non-human animal should never be consumed. This indicates God places high value on the life of non-human animals in addition to humans.

Mark 7:1-23 – "The Source of Your Pollution"

"The Pharisees, along with some religion scholars who had come from Jerusalem, gathered around him. They noticed that some of his disciples weren't being careful with ritual washings before meals. The Pharisees—Jews in general, in fact—would never eat a meal without going through the motions of a ritual hand-washing, with an especially vigorous scrubbing if they had just come from the market (to say nothing of the scouring they'd give jugs and pots and pans).

5 The Pharisees and religion scholars asked, "Why do your disciples flout the rules, showing up at meals without washing their hands?" 6-8 Jesus answered, "Isaiah was right about frauds like you, hit the bull's-eye in fact: These people make a big show of saying the right thing, but their heart isn't in it.

They act like they are worshiping me, but they don't mean it. They just use me as a cover for teaching whatever suits their fancy, Ditching God's command and taking up the latest fads."

9-13 He went on, "Well, good for you. You get rid of God's command so you won't be inconvenienced in following the religious fashions! Moses said, 'Respect your father and mother,' and, 'Anyone denouncing father or mother should be killed.' But you weasel out of that by saying that it's perfectly acceptable to say to father or mother, 'Gift! What I owed you I've given as a gift to God,' thus relieving yourselves of obligation to father or mother. You scratch out God's Word and scrawl a whim in its place. You do a lot of things like this."

14-15 Jesus called the crowd together again and said, "Listen now, all of you—take this to heart. *It's not what you swallow that pollutes your life; it's what you vomit—that's the real pollution.*"
17 When he was back home after being with the crowd, his disciples said, "We don't get it. Put it in plain language."

18-19 Jesus said, "Are you being willfully stupid? Don't you see that what you swallow can't contaminate you? It doesn't enter your heart but your stomach, works its way through the intestines, and is finally flushed." (That took care of dietary quibbling; Jesus was saying that *all* foods are fit to eat.)

20-23 He went on: "It's what comes out of a person that pollutes: obscenities, lusts, thefts, murders, adulteries, greed, depravity, deceptive dealings, carousing, mean looks, slander, arrogance, foolishness—all these are vomit from the heart. *There* is the source of your pollution."

(Emphases mine, MSG translation)

Here in Mark 7, Jesus is talking with some Pharisees who have an insane obsession with trying to "be clean before God." He calls them out for their hypocrisy, saying that their food rituals are useless because their hearts are dirty before God. Jesus says they shouldn't be so obsessed with their food if their internal righteousness is absent. Jesus' disciples then wrongly take his words to mean that some foods are okay while others are not. Jesus later calls out his disciples for their error and says all foods are fit to eat. **Not beneficial; acceptable.**

So using Mark 7 as an argument to eat meat is rather pointless, because the Jesus/Pharisees/disciples conversation is about internal cleanliness, not about what to eat.

Can you eat meat and still be a Christian? Yes. Should you? Not by my summation. Using Mark 7 as justification for non-human animal consumption of any kind is a blatant sidestep of all other factors in the Bible and, most importantly, how we treat billions of non-human animals every year while claiming to be a "developed" or "humane" species.

This brings me to another point: people today love to use past times as reasons and examples to eat meat. Yet, for all intents and purposes, we do not live in a world where food is scarce anymore, or with limited choices. There are more food products today than ever and we produce enough food to feed 10 billion people.* The point is, people compare Bible times where there were limited food options to the present day where we have more food options than we could ever count. And we still kill 150+ billion non-human animals a year for taste, pleasure and profit. It is a completely ludicrous comparison.

Didn't God Provide Quail For Humans To Eat?

Numbers 11:1-34

11 **1-3** "The people fell to grumbling over their hard life. GOD heard. When he heard his anger flared; then fire blazed up and burned the outer boundaries of the camp. The people cried out for help to Moses; Moses prayed to GOD and the fire died down. They named the place Taberah (Blaze) because fire from GOD had blazed up against them.

4-6 "The riffraff among the people had a craving and soon they had the People of Israel whining, "Why can't we have meat? We ate fish in Egypt—and got it free!—to say nothing of the cucumbers and melons, the leeks and onions and garlic. But nothing tastes good out here; all we get is manna, manna, manna."

7-9 "Manna was a seedlike substance with a shiny appearance like resin. The people went around collecting it and ground it between stones or pounded it fine in a mortar. Then they boiled it in a pot and shaped it into cakes. It tasted like a delicacy cooked in olive oil. When the dew fell on the camp at night, the manna was right there with it.

10 "Moses heard the whining, all those families whining in front of their tents. GOD's anger blazed up. Moses saw that things were in a bad way. **11-15** Moses said to GOD, "Why are you treating me this way? What did I ever do to you to deserve this? Did I conceive them? Was I their mother? So why dump the responsibility of this people on me? Why tell me to carry them around like a nursing mother, carry them all the way to the land you promised to their ancestors? Where am I supposed to get meat for all these people who are whining to me, 'Give us meat; we want meat.' I can't do this by myself—it's too much, all these people. If this is how you intend to treat me, do me a favor and kill me. I've seen enough; I've had enough. Let me out of here."

¹⁶-¹⁷ "GOD said to Moses, 'Gather together seventy men from among the leaders of Israel, men whom you know to be respected and responsible. Take them to the Tent of Meeting. I'll meet you there. I'll come down and speak with you. I'll take some of the Spirit that is on you and place it on them; they'll then be able to take some of the load of this people—you won't have to carry the whole thing alone.

¹⁸-²⁰ "'Tell the people, Consecrate yourselves. Get ready for tomorrow when you're going to eat meat. You've been whining to GOD, 'We want meat; give us meat. We had a better life in Egypt.' GOD has heard your whining and he's going to give you meat. You're going to eat meat. And it's not just for a day that you'll eat meat, and not two days, or five or ten or twenty, but for a whole month. You're going to eat meat until it's coming out your nostrils. You're going to be so sick of meat that you'll throw up at the mere mention of it. And here's why: Because you have rejected GOD who is right here among you, whining to his face, 'Oh, why did we ever have to leave Egypt?'"

²¹-²² 'Moses said, "I'm standing here surrounded by 600,000 men on foot and you say, 'I'll give them meat, meat every day for a month.' So where's it coming from? Even if all the flocks and herds were butchered, would that be enough? Even if all the fish in the sea were caught, would that be enough?"

23 "God answered Moses, "So, do you think I can't take care of you? You'll see soon enough whether what I say happens for you or not." **24-25** So Moses went out and told the people what God had said. He called together seventy of the leaders and had them stand around the Tent. God came down in a cloud and spoke to Moses and took some of the Spirit that was on him and put it on the seventy leaders. When the Spirit rested on them they prophesied. But they didn't continue; it was a onetime event.

26 "Meanwhile two men, Eldad and Medad, had stayed in the camp. They were listed as leaders but they didn't leave camp to go to the Tent. Still, the Spirit also rested on them and they prophesied in the camp. **27** A young man ran and told Moses, "Eldad and Medad are prophesying in the camp!" **28** Joshua son of Nun, who had been Moses' right-hand man since his youth, said, "Moses, master! Stop them!" **29** But Moses said, "Are you jealous for me? Would that all God's people were prophets. Would that God would put his Spirit on all of them."

30-34 "Then Moses and the leaders of Israel went back to the camp. A wind set in motion by God swept quails in from the sea. They piled up to a depth of about three feet in the camp and as far out as a day's walk in every direction. All that day and night and into the next day the people were out gathering the quail—huge amounts of quail; even the slowest person among them gathered at least sixty bushels. They spread them out all over the camp for drying. But while they were still chewing the quail and had hardly swallowed the first bites, God's anger blazed out against the people. He hit them with a terrible plague. They ended up calling the place Kibroth Hattaavah

(Graves-of-the-Craving). There they buried the people who craved meat."

With this story, as Samuel Barger puts it, it's important to know *why* something happened, not just *what* happened. If you notice in Numbers 11, the Israelites are speaking from hard hearts, not grateful and compassionate ones. They request meat in this hard-hearted state, and God gives it to them – probably not because God was pleased with their request, but because He wanted to give them a "taste of their own medicine," if you will. "'All things are lawful,' but not all things are helpful. 'All things are lawful,' but not all things build up" (1 Corinthians 10:23, ESV).

We should not ask for non-human animal food or seek it out just because it's permitted. Just because we have the power or permission to do something doesn't automatically qualify it as a righteous action.

We cannot overlook the violence, neglect, torture and abuse we shove towards non-human animals, all in the name of taste, tradition, habit and convenience – especially not if we claim to be Christians. Justice, peace, grace and love are just as important to show to non-human animals as they are to humans. It's hypocrisy to pet a cat in your house and eat a pig on your dinner plate.

Didn't God Command Elijah To Sacrifice A Non-Human Animal?

God didn't command Elijah to do this; not by any stretch of the word. If you read that section in 1 Kings, the bull sacrifice was Elijah's idea. God never commanded him to do that. God responded to a human's (Elijah's) idea and faithful (albeit imperfect) devotion, but the bull sacrifice was not even remotely God's command.

Going back to what Paul said in 1 Corinthians: "Looking at it one way, you could say, 'Anything goes. Because of God's immense generosity and grace, we don't have to dissect and scrutinize every action to see if it will pass muster.' But the point is not to just get by. We want to live well, but our foremost efforts should be to help others live well." - 1 Corinthians 10:23-24, MSG translation

Didn't Jesus Eat Fish?

In John 21, we witness Jesus allegedly taking fish and making breakfast out of it.

After a painstakingly meticulous historical analysis, we find it is unlikely Jesus ever consumed fish. The word "fish" itself was not known merely as a creature or source of food in early Christianity. It was best known as a symbol for Jesus Christ – the Messiah – Himself. Fish translates to "ichthys" in Greek, which is an acronym that represents "savior, son of God, or Jesus Christ."*

Was Jesus Actually A Vegetarian?

From all the available data, ruthless historical analysis of early Christian texts, Biblical hermeneutics and careful consideration of past and current Christian values, yes – we find with nearly complete certainty that Jesus was a vegetarian.*

Jesus' brother James was raised and remained a vegetarian. We know this from *Ecclesiastical History* by Eusebius, bishop of Caesarea.

In the early church, there were also small groups of Christians who took the stance that meat eating was a matter of conscience, not of preference. This was invariably another reality in which vegetarianism/veganism held ground in early Christianity but was later challenged by those who sought to place individual satisfaction above righteous living.

Isaiah 25:6

Praise to the LORD

25 "LORD, you are my God;
    I will exalt you and praise your name,
for in perfect faithfulness
    you have done wonderful things,
    things planned long ago.
2 You have made the city a heap of rubble,
    the fortified town a ruin,
the foreigners' stronghold a city no more;
    it will never be rebuilt.
3 Therefore strong peoples will honor you;
    cities of ruthless nations will revere you.
4 You have been a refuge for the poor,
    a refuge for the needy in their distress,
a shelter from the storm
    and a shade from the heat.
For the breath of the ruthless
    is like a storm driving against a wall
5   and like the heat of the desert.
You silence the uproar of foreigners;

as heat is reduced by the shadow of a cloud,
   so the song of the ruthless is stilled.
6 On this mountain the LORD Almighty will prepare
   a feast of rich food for all peoples,
a banquet of aged wine—
   the best of meats and the finest of wines.
7 On this mountain he will destroy
   the shroud that enfolds all peoples,
the sheet that covers all nations;
8   he will swallow up death forever.
The Sovereign LORD will wipe away the tears
   from all faces;
he will remove his people's disgrace
   from all the earth.
The LORD has spoken." (NIV translation)

Christians will occasionally bring up Isaiah 25:6 as a verse supporting the consumption of meat and non-human animal products. The verse indeed appears lucid and without any ambiguity – Isaiah's description of the future for the people of Israel describes "choice meat and wine" as dinner to look forward to.

Based on the research I've done relevant to this passage,* there's no need to hide the fact that delicacies such as animal products and alcoholic beverages were desires and realities in Bible times (as they are today). Christ-followers who are eager to dine on fatty meat and aged wine readily cite Isaiah 25:6 as their "ticket to an animal-foods-filled feast." But, just like any other passage in the Bible – especially those that can lead to divisive discourse – we must take words within context and within the framework of the people who a passage is relevant to.

Throughout the entire preceding chapter (Isaiah 24), we read of God's wrath being poured out upon the Israelites for their wrongdoings against and straying from God:

Isaiah 24: The LORD's Devastation of the Earth

24 "See, the LORD is going to lay waste the earth
  and devastate it;
he will ruin its face
  and scatter its inhabitants—
² it will be the same
  for priest as for people,
  for the master as for his servant,
  for the mistress as for her servant,
  for seller as for buyer,
  for borrower as for lender,
  for debtor as for creditor.
³ The earth will be completely laid waste
  and totally plundered.
The LORD has spoken this word.
⁴ The earth dries up and withers,
  the world languishes and withers,
  the heavens languish with the earth.
⁵ The earth is defiled by its people;
  they have disobeyed the laws,
violated the statutes
  and broken the everlasting covenant.
⁶ Therefore a curse consumes the earth;
  its people must bear their guilt.
Therefore earth's inhabitants are burned up,
  and very few are left.
⁷ The new wine dries up and the vine withers;
  all the merrymakers groan.
⁸ The joyful timbrels are stilled,

the noise of the revelers has stopped,
    the joyful harp is silent.
9 No longer do they drink wine with a song;
    the beer is bitter to its drinkers.
10 The ruined city lies desolate;
    the entrance to every house is barred.
11 In the streets they cry out for wine;
    all joy turns to gloom,
    all joyful sounds are banished from the earth.
12 The city is left in ruins,
    its gate is battered to pieces.
13 So will it be on the earth
    and among the nations,
as when an olive tree is beaten,
    or as when gleanings are left after the grape
harvest." (NIV translation)

After reading this chapter, it's clear God is delivering justice towards unholy actions. Since God is a perfect, just and holy God, He cannot permit sin or any kind of disobedience around Him. People are free to reject God but that results in being without God's life, hope and blessings. Isaiah 24 is a perfect example of the temporary loss of hope.

In Bible times, resources were scarce and this included wine and non-human animal products. The number of non-human animals and amount of land owned by a family was often directly related to that family's wealth, and as such, the delicacies of one's resources (read: meats and wines) were used under specific conditions only. Festivals, celebrations, weddings, reunions, hosting guests and other such events were primary designations for the use of delicacies.

As such, Israelites (and dozens of other surrounding peoples) were all too accustomed to saving the richest foods for rare occasions and rationing normal food supplies as a result. It was considered poor taste and judgement to over-utilize scarce goods when they could be saved for truly necessary circumstances.

Therefore, it's only natural for the Israelites (and others) to revere foods such as meat and wine as the "feast foods" that they are. Incidentally, not much has changed across the years – America still regards meat and wine (among other indulgences) as celebratory-level food. Sadly, due to America's consumeristic predictability and patent inclinations towards the biggest and best of everything, wine and meat are not reserved for the rarest of moments – they are roughly as common as any suburban house party. In other words, since edible and monetary resources are not as rare as they once were, here in America we over-abundantly partake in food that we arbitrarily produce for our own ends.

Isaiah himself had already declared a "fearless, deathless" Heaven. We see this in Isaiah 11:6-9 (prior to 24 and 25):

The wolf will live with the lamb,
   the leopard will lie down with the goat,
the calf and the lion and the yearling together;
   and a little child will lead them.
7 The cow will feed with the bear,
   their young will lie down together,
   and the lion will eat straw like the ox.
8 The infant will play near the cobra's den,
   and the young child will put its hand into the
viper's nest.

⁹ They will neither harm nor destroy
  on all my holy mountain,
for the earth will be filled with the knowledge of
the LORD
  as the waters cover the sea.

And, according to all the links and similarities between Eden and the New Heaven, a deathless environment invariably includes non-human animals. Since non-human animals were not required for human food in Eden, certainly they would not be on the menu in Heaven.

As has become clear through a contextual analysis of this passage, the word "meat" is simply used to refer to completely rich, filling and rare food – not the exploitation of non-human animals.

John 2:13-17

¹³⁻¹⁴ "When the Passover Feast, celebrated each spring by the Jews, was about to take place, Jesus traveled up to Jerusalem. He found the Temple teeming with people selling cattle and sheep and doves. The loan sharks were also there in full strength.

¹⁵⁻¹⁷ "Jesus put together a whip out of strips of leather and chased them out of the Temple, stampeding the sheep and cattle, upending the tables of the loan sharks, spilling coins left and right.

"He told the dove merchants, 'Get your things out of here! Stop turning my Father's house into a shopping mall!' That's when his disciples remembered the Scripture, 'Zeal for your house consumes me.'"

Here is another example where Jesus Himself made a conspicuously, even painfully obvious declaration that the exploitation of non-human animals is wrong. The merchants, traders and tax collectors of the time were known for both utilizing every business opportunity available and overcharging people for transactions. These were patently maligned uses of the Temple and Jesus knew He had to make a public statement about it. Not only was He frustrated about the oppression of non-human animals, He was infuriated that the people of the time (as a larger group) permitted it to happen as publically and long as it did.

Christianity, Non-Human Animal Consumption And Consumerism: From Past To Present

It is a convenient idea to think that in former times, people had better hearts and no ounce of consumerism (or anything similar) was present. Yet, this can be refuted again and again; plus, we don't even need to look further than the Bible (unless we want to).

King Solomon himself is the perfect example. Here, I borrow his words directly from Ecclesiastes:

Ecclesiastes 1:12-14

[12-14] "Call me 'the Quester.' I've been king over Israel in Jerusalem. I looked most carefully into everything, searched out all that is done on this earth. And let me tell you, there's not much to write home about. God hasn't made it easy for us. I've seen it all and it's nothing but smoke—smoke, and spitting into the wind."

Solomon goes on to further cement his point that even all the world's pleasure couldn't fill him up:

Ecclesiastes 2:1-10

1-3 "I said to myself, 'Let's go for it—experiment with pleasure, have a good time!' But there was nothing to it, nothing but smoke.
What do I think of the fun-filled life? Insane! Inane!
My verdict on the pursuit of happiness? Who needs it?

"With the help of a bottle of wine
   and all the wisdom I could muster,
I tried my level best
   to penetrate the absurdity of life.
I wanted to get a handle on anything useful we mortals might do
   during the years we spend on this earth.

4-8 "Oh, I did great things:
   built houses,
   planted vineyards,
   designed gardens and parks
      and planted a variety of fruit trees in them,
   made pools of water
      to irrigate the groves of trees.
I bought slaves, male and female,
      who had children, giving me even more slaves;
   then I acquired large herds and flocks,
      larger than any before me in Jerusalem.
I piled up silver and gold,
      loot from kings and kingdoms.
I gathered a chorus of singers to entertain me with song,

and—most exquisite of all pleasures—
voluptuous maidens for my bed.
⁹⁻¹⁰ Oh, how I prospered! I left all my predecessors in
Jerusalem far behind, left them behind in the dust.
What's more, I kept a clear head through it all.
"Everything I wanted I took—I never said no to
myself. I gave in to every impulse, held back nothing. I
sucked the marrow of pleasure out of every task—my
reward to myself for a hard day's work!"

Ecclesiastes 2:11 – "I Hate Life"

¹¹ "Then I took a good look at everything I'd done,
looked at all the sweat and hard work. But when I
looked, I saw nothing but smoke. Smoke and spitting
into the wind. There was nothing to any of it.
Nothing."

If one of the richest men of all time pursued literally
every desire that even temporarily lingered within his
heart and failed to find meaning or purpose within it,
it should be a sign to all of us (especially Christians)
that **consumerism is deadly.**

After reflecting on these passages, it's clear to us that
consumerism – the drive for constant accumulation
and consumption of more things – was passed down
through the ages, and has done everything but
disappear. Even more accurately, consumerism is
simply a tangible tendency that has roots deep within
human nature. As societal structures and economic
interests have risen and developed, organizations of
people have only hungered more ravenously for more
cash – a metric that falls humiliatingly short of life's
true meaning.

Beyond simple economic speculation, consumerism has worked its way into Christian culture. Christians (as we [admittedly] know ourselves today) are perhaps the saddest example of food consumerism ingrained within another culture. We accept and even encourage junk food as though it is a simple choice devoid of consequences – roughly as meaningful as the clothes we choose to wear each day.

The drive to constantly have more and more simply won't yield the results we as Christians claim we want; not just for ourselves but for the entire world. It's a sign of the times indeed when we apprehensively or glumly accept conditions that secular food culture attempts to uphold instead of ruthlessly examining and reevaluating every sort of systemic consumerist agenda we are greeted with (more on this later in the book).

In order for subsequent points to make sense, I'd like to break down the macrocosm of non-human animal consumerism from a temporarily secular worldview. If you were born and raised in a country or city that is financially and economically better off than other areas of the world, chances are you've rarely had to worry about what you'll eat, or why. The bigger questions are typically who are you going to eat with and where.

Take my own story as an example. For 19 years, I lived a "food" life in the same fashion as the rest of my peers and (generally speaking) cultural background. I consumed meat, cheese, dairy and eggs just like my friends, loved essentially everything about them, and not for a minute did I question anything. I was fed the same lies that all of us have been fed one point or another: Your animal products come from farms that grow happy non-human animals who have lived full, free lives – until the end of their lives, that is. They've never been confined, they've been fed a nutritious, antibiotic-free diet, and most importantly, they've given of their lives so *you* can have sound nutrition and not go hungry.

As we now know, nothing could be further from the truth. **Absolutely *nothing*.** While the majority of this book is a veganism and justice apologetics book for the Christian, this section warrants a bit more explanation about modern-day animal treatment.

Cows, pigs, chickens, sheep, fish and other sentient non-human animals used for food are subjected to a miserably brief life of abject torture, imprisonment and death. The global level of non-human animal consumerism has risen to such a degree that we now slaughter 150 billion non-human animals every year (this includes sea animals). This number does not include bykill or accidental deaths; it only includes the numbers of non-human animals bred and slaughtered for taste.

This is such a horrifically high number that, when one truly contemplates it, such a premise openly and deafeningly demands an answer: **For what ultimate purpose do humans persist in this utterly barbaric and wasteful practice?**

Isn't Christian History And Culture At Odds With Veganism?

Many assume (myself included at one point) that veganism and Christianity are two causes that couldn't be more appropriately polarized to each other. In other words, United States pop culture at large often associates vegetarianism and veganism with individuals and subcultures that would rarely (if ever) find themselves in a Christian church building or engaging in "religious behaviors or activities."

In truth, non-human animal rights activists and veganism found many roots in Christianity before there were ever left-wing surges in non-human animal activism, veganism or advocacy for vegan-related causes and movements.

"I was convinced that God had called me to devote whatever advantages He might have bestowed upon me to the cause of the weak, the helpless, both man and beast, and those who had none to help them."

– Anthony Ashley Cooper, Earl of Shaftesbury

"We may pretend to what religion we please, but cruelty is atheism. We may boast of Christianity; but cruelty is infidelity. We may trust our orthodoxy; but cruelty is the worst of heresies."

– Humphrey Primatt, Anglican priest, from *A Dissertation on the Duty of Mercy and the Sin of Cruelty to Brute Animals*

"Animals are God's creatures, not human property, nor utilities, nor resources, nor commodities, but precious beings in God's sight.... Christians whose eyes are fixed on the awfulness of crucifixion are in a special position to understand the awfulness of innocent suffering. The Cross of Christ is God's absolute identification with the weak, the powerless, and the vulnerable, but most of all with unprotected, undefended, innocent suffering."

– Andrew Linzey, PhD, DD

"Animals have done us no harm and they have no power of resistance. Cruelty to animals is as if man did not love God. There is something so very dreadful, so satanic, in tormenting those who have never harmed us, who cannot defend themselves, who are utterly in our power, who have weapons neither of offence nor defense, that none but very hardened persons can endure the thought of it."

– Cardinal John Henry Newman

"Oh, God, enlarge within us the sense of fellowship with all living things, our brothers and the animals to whom Thou gavest the Earth in common with us. We remember with shame that in the past we have exercised the high dominion of man with ruthless cruelty so that the voice of the Earth, which should have gone up to Thee in song, has been a groan of travail."

– Saint Basil, bishop of Caesarea

"What is a charitable heart?

"It is a heart which is burning with love for the whole creation, for men, for the birds, for the beasts... for all creatures. He who has such a heart cannot see or call to mind a creature without his eyes being filled with tears by reason of the immense compassion which seizes his heart; a heart which is softened and can no longer bear to see or learn from others of any suffering, even the smallest pain being inflicted upon a creature. That is why such a man never ceases to pray for the animals... moved by the infinite pity which reigns in the hearts of those who are becoming united with God."

– Saint Isaac the Syrian

What Do We Do Now/How Do We Make Sense Of The Big Picture/How Do We Handle Contradictions, Real Or Supposed?

Throughout this chapter, all of the information presented may have easily become too overwhelming. This is completely understandable – as not only is there a lot, there are areas of this chapter alone that may have appeared contradictory.

I freely admit that while I put hundreds of hours into researching material, books, facts and blogs for this work, I have not answered every question a Christian or non-Christian may have about non-human animal consumption and how it fits (or doesn't fit) into

Christianity. The biggest takeaway from this chapter is the following:

Individual and group relationships will come and go in your life, but at the end of the day, you have to ask yourself what values, principles and characteristics you already hold, and how your existing motivations and behaviors can fit into a framework that holistically builds a more compassionate lifestyle for yourself and all you meet.

Chapter 2 Thesis:

True Christianity both intrinsically represents vegan values and reveals dozens of direct Scriptural citations and Bible accounts that unambiguously paint God's original design for Earth as vegan. Despite any seeming contradictions or personal reluctance, the committed Christian must embrace veganism as a beneficial, freedom-inducing, suitable lifestyle for all. The Christian must unabashedly reject consumerism, cultural prevarications, cognitive blind spots, comfort-perpetuating traditions and any Christian scripts that prevent action-oriented compassion from happening and growing.

"I prefer to be true to myself, even at the hazard of incurring the ridicule of others, rather than to be false, and to incur my own abhorrence." – Frederick Douglass, American abolitionist

Chapter 3: Connecting Opportunities For Compassion

"The three hardest tasks in the world are neither physical feats nor intellectual achievements, but moral acts: to return love for hate, to include the excluded, and to say, 'I was wrong.'" – Sydney J. Harris, *Pieces Of Eight*

The Story Of Josh King

In 1991, Josh King was born in the small town of St. Marys, Ohio. Because the birth was two weeks late and exacerbated by meconium aspiration – the accidental inhalation of fecal matter – as a neonate he was pronounced dead.

Fortunately, the story did not end there – not by a *long shot*. Josh King not only survived his unfortunate birth circumstances, he pushed ahead to become a first-generation college graduate with a degree he was extremely passionate about. But it wasn't smooth sailing all the way through.

Young King found an interest in sports, and specifically sports equipment from a young age. He began working in his high school's equipment room while still a student there – building experience and knowledge from the ground up.

Even though his dream was to one day walk the graduation stage at a notable college, he discounted this option while still young, and instead enrolled within a branch of Wright State University, a public college in Fairborn, Ohio.

While working towards a career as a police officer at Wright, King couldn't get the idea of sports equipment management out of his head – or his heart. King kept looking and sure enough, he found a sports management program at Bowling Green State University in Bowling Green, Ohio. This new endeavor took full precedence in his life from that point forward, and Josh King became more invigorated than ever.

In 2014, King reached the point where he was only days away from graduation and beginning a successful career. All who know him personally have praised his unmatched work ethic, persistence and ability to remain joyful despite all kinds of obstacles.

To the typical reader, this story is likely encouraging but not necessarily remarkable – until you discover more about what Josh King had to overcome. In order to resuscitate King, six nurses and three doctors had to perform over-the-top lifesaving acts, and even afterwards, King was kept in an incubator for weeks after his birth to ensure healthy progress.

The lifesaving conditions and actions that Josh King was administered left him scarred by a host of learning disabilities and mild cerebral palsy. His quest to become a sports equipment manager was tested by these setbacks, which at the very least tested his level of ambition beyond high school graduation.

It is easy to think Josh's story matters when you read about it and get to know him better through that. And of course Josh's story matters, just like everyone else's. But to simply acknowledge Josh's story as significant and then move on to the next thing is to miss the main point.

Stories feel as though they hold greater significance when we see and hear them up close. In other words, all stories matter, but we don't get to see or hear many of them – especially with non-human animals – because we don't have the context through which to witness them, or because we simply don't pay attention.

LGBTQ Communities And The Need For Compassion

As I was drafting this part of the book, I kept realizing that I was adding ideas to a chapter that ultimately I wouldn't have as much experience speaking on as I do with the other chapters. So, this is the multifaceted conclusion I came to...

- I have a number of LGBTQ friends, and we get along quite well. This is due to sincerity from both parties.

- LGBTQ people are vastly misunderstood – not because they make no effort to share information about themselves, but because heterosexuals often make little to no effort to understand the LGBTQ folks among us or even give them the time of day. It's high time this changed.

- I could try to write a chapter on how LGBTQ communities and veganism are similar and connected (and there are indeed dozens of similarities), but since I do not have as much knowledge here as I do other areas, I am not going to write a chapter full of fluff and rhetoric.

The remainder of this chapter will be an overview of a few quick truths and practical steps Christians, those looking to become vegan and Christian vegans can take to create greater harmony and truer depth of relationships with the LGBTQ community. The media already skews the hard work of Christians; let's not mess that up further. We have to get our internal act together if others are going to take us seriously.

Love Has Been Replaced By Legalism

Legalism cannot be more important than love. When possible, it is most admirable to combine truth with deep love, but love must come first. We should be more concerned about doing things right than doing the right thing. It is the position of your heart that matters most, not your method.

One Crucial Step On The Path To Forming A Permanently Vegan World Is Re-Instilling The Fundamentals Of Community

What are the true fundamentals of community? Bill Hybels' definition is my favorite:

"To know and be known;
To love and be loved;
To serve and be served;
To celebrate and be celebrated."

We must spend time together again: learning, sharing, giving, celebrating, mourning, discussing, asking, planning, acting and loving. Community is about celebrating what it means to be human, sharing that with others and providing support when and how necessary for still-developing communities.

Connecting The Seemingly Disconnected

Historically, humans have struggled to connect with non-human animals or give them their freedoms, largely because **we selfishly neglect to appreciate their differentness without exploiting them.**

We often look at non-human animals outside our zone of familiarity and think little to nothing of them – **not because they have no value, but because we take no time to see it.**

Funnily enough, humans are some of the lowest creatures God made. We see this clearly in Charles Camosy's lucid explanation of various creatures God has created, and their general place in the universe.* Non-human animals are expressly called *good* by God before humans are even walking the Earth. It's for this reason and many more that humans have no right to take the lives of non-human animals.

So much of our perceived inability to connect deeper with non-human animals that aren't cats, dogs and other common house pets is because we just don't spend time with them. We grow up receiving cues about how life is supposed to go when involving non-human animals without taking time to question the root of such cues.

Take the family traveling to the local zoo for a day as an example. Let's say it's a father, mother, son and daughter, and since the father has limited time off during the year, the family wants to maximize time spent together. The parents choose a recreational activity that will satiate the children without requiring too much in the way of planning. Thusly, the zoo is chosen as suitable for all.

Once reaching the zoo, it's a common occurrence to see exotic non-human animals at every turn. Lions, tigers and bears are frequent features at zoos, and indeed – unless an individual has the means to travel abroad, these non-human animals and more are unlikely to be seen in "real life."

Zoos, for the most part, do a fairly good job at hanging educational placards or information booklets around their facilities. These help people learn more about such rare and precious non-human animals, and at least heighten some gratitude and appreciation for them. But the area zoos, aquariums and similar attractions fall short is glaring: we don't truly value non-human animals, their freedom and all the diversity they add to the world if we seek to confine them.

We often treat non-human animals as merely objects on display, or property with which we can meet our selfish ends. We rarely, if ever, consider how a non-human animal's intrinsic desire for a free life can be fulfilled without any loss to us – or for its own valuable sake. Indeed, the irony is severe; by removing the freedom of other non-human animals, we are slowly removing our own freedom. By failing to support the freedom of creatures less like us, we are failing to support the freedom of our own kind.

These collective choices that establish the fabric of our present world cause a massive moral dilemma that most people don't notice until a few particular events or circumstances take place. We "want" all non-human animals to be free, but we rarely perform our due diligence surrounding why non-human animals have particular, rightful places in our world.

While driving along a road, if one individual were to see another ruthlessly beating a dog to death with a baseball bat, you can bet with 99 percent certainty police officers would be on the scene within minutes, because someone would have called about the violence. While the bystander effect has been proven true countless times, few people allow non-human animals – especially those we're familiar with – to be openly abused in such a way.

Yet, the exact same person who called the police on the dog murderer might pull into a fast food queue minutes later, to purchase a chicken sandwich or perhaps a burger. There's no consideration over the food choice because the process in which the innocent chicken's flesh arrived packaged as such is completely hidden from plain observation.

We think vile thoughts towards those who publically mistreat non-human animals we're familiar with, and we think nothing of "business as usual" – ordering a cheeseburger, fries and soft drink with friends on the weekend.

The catch? These actions are morally equivalent. If a punishment-worthy owner bludgeons a harmless Labrador to death and a factory farm worker mercilessly stabs a harmless pig in the throat so it can be made into "food," the only disparity here is our perception as a society.

When taking a step back to view the facts, you'd be hard-pressed to find an individual that would claim one of these actions is okay and another is not. Many individuals rush to speculate and query about the levels of "humane" treatment within slaughterhouses and farms, attempting to somehow justify the mistreatment of thousands of non-human animals on a daily basis. Cognitive dissonance hurts, no questions there. When some form of comfort is at stake for our own lives, we seek to uphold the status quo instead of questioning what's really happening – even if questioning is the moral, just thing to do.

The meat industry understands all this, which is precisely why they work so hard and pay so well to hide all the evidence of their carnage. We're practically inundated with all the opposite – images, videos, copywriting and even sample scents on a daily basis, inviting us to take part in the latest "delicious" trend. Grocery stores, restaurants, product packaging, commercials and our own family and friends frequently perpetuate the idea that non-human animal foods are acceptable, correct, desirable and praiseworthy.

There are companies such as Chick-fil-A which make a farce out of the whole thing. Throughout their marketing, they often have cows suggesting to consumers to "Eat mor chikin," as though the choice between cow and chicken meat is an inconvenience in an otherwise innocuous landscape of non-human animal products. In fact, I'd say the only type of media messaging the typical consumer receives more often than those relating to food are those pertaining to sex.

Another reason we feel separated from the vast majority of animals is because we have natural language barriers. Pigs cannot speak human languages, at least as far as we know, and we cannot speak pig. However, this does not bar any human from compassion – the behaviors, thoughts and actions associated with lifting others out of misery and preserving their wellbeing.

But even this is an excuse. Dogs, cats, fish, hamsters

and lizards cannot speak English or any other human language (from what we know), but this does not mean they are not sentient nor have their own languages. It all comes back full circle to the familiarity factor. We place arbitrary value on specific non-human animals that have "more to offer us," and we commodify those we decide are less valuable.

We don't have the freedom to decide what's right for other species; we simply have to support and nurture their freedom.

The Elderly

The elderly are often neglected as "unproductive" members of society who are experiencing cognitive and physical decline. While decline is inevitable, lack of activity and simply enjoying life are not.

Regardless, the fact stands that the elderly are some of the most overlooked members of society anywhere. As people age, their social circles diminish, engaging programs are sometimes fewer and keeping up the former quality of life is a struggle.

Yet, few would argue that the elderly are not important. In fact, everyone I can think of personally has respect and reverence for the elderly. Grandparents, teachers, veterans and other personal roles come to mind. So how come we as a society have such a difficult time handling and interacting with elders?

Is it because oftentimes, we feel uncomfortable around them. Baby Boomers and preceding generations did not grow up with the technology available today, so conversations, daily activities and outings take on different forms and social meetings. Their attention spans are longer which means they are able to hold conversations longer (this is not a bad thing). Sometimes memory problems creep in, and this complicates matters. Indeed, the Centers for Disease Control and Prevention report that roughly 83,000 individuals die from Alzheimer's every year, and 5 million more people in the United States alone are living with it daily.

So what do we do? We spend more time with them and offer suggestions for activities. We must document their experiences. We must simply be with them and get to know them.

We don't have to assume we know all the answers; in truth, this won't always happen. We also don't need to worry about providing perfect solutions all the time. But in order to serve the overlooked and oppressed, we must observe them, care for them, give them our best and allow them to be their fullest, brightest selves. Darkening another's life more often causes trouble when we overlook their basic rights to certain freedoms. We don't need to worry about getting things perfect from the get-go; our primary concern must rest in protecting and uplifting experiences of freedom for those who may have otherwise never experienced it.

Compassion As A Lifestyle

Over recent decades, dozens of trends (both secular and Christian) have come and gone, each leaving its mark on culture as we know it. Despite real-life victims and survivors of breast cancer openly speaking out against it (I support them in their disapproval and anger), the pink ribbon of breast cancer awareness has remained one of the most visually prominent marketing efforts of recent memory. In 2004, the Livestrong Foundation began a marketing effort in which bright yellow bracelets with the company's name upon them were sold with profits being used to benefit the lives of cancer patients. What's even worse here is that only six years later, Lance Armstrong – then chairman and board member of Livestrong – was found a cheater and a liar, having used banned drugs to improve his cycling performance.

It's crazy that these things happened; it's crazy that these stories are true. They are powerful illustrations that some of the most iconic and memorable movements can still cause pain for everyday people or be affected by the poor choices of certain individuals. All of this is to discuss a specific point. Most people are likely to hop on the bandwagon if the conditions are right. If an action or event is "for a good cause," people see their friends doing it and there's no deeper thought required for being involved, the average person would gladly step aboard.

What's far rarer is witnessing individuals live their entire lives producing actions that revolve around firmly rooted convictions or principles. For example, if asked, most people would readily associate themselves with concern for the environment. Yet, how many people can you think of (off the top of your head) who fastidiously and even strategically take actions that readily improve the global environment?

Similarly, most people would say they love animals

and are against animal abuse. Yet, how many people can you think of who, with as many daily actions as they can reasonably take, truly improve the lives of as many non-human animals as possible?

These can sound like overwhelming, even difficult questions. And from one vantage point, they are. But if we are to address these questions from the most logical standpoint, I find we'll reach a conclusion that is simpler albeit uncomfortable, at times. Throughout the rest of this book we will examine what is required for this type of lifestyle.

Love, grace, kindness and compassion are universally accepted as primary and essential Christian values. I've never met or known anyone who would press against these virtues, or claim they are futile. Yet, true love is not always convenient, easy or palatable; that is precisely why it is love.

Love is an action far more than it is a feeling. It is also a matter of consistency far more than it is just taking action based off a moment of inspiration. Love pushes past the good and fights for the best. Love is defined by persistence, commitment, quality, effort, faith, hope and sacrifice.

How To Develop And Utilize A Wise, Discerning Mind

I don't have to write at length for nearly everyone to agree that the world is not currently in a splendid state.

Harking back to non-human animal consumerism, we understand that a consumerist culture has weaseled its way into Christian culture. Unless you already make an effort to be highly discerning and observant in your daily choices as a consumer, chances are you take actions every day that have been programmed. Now I'm not trying to go all Neo/Morpheus/Matrix on you. But The Matrix is eerily accurate when it comes to being a perfect analogy for the situation we face today.

We live in a culture where non-human animal consumption and exploitation is assumed, preconceived and taken as normal in nearly all regards – yet still arbitrarily chosen. For example, dogs and cats are upheld as some of the shining beacons of non-human animals worthy of affection, whereas dozens of others are exploited at will, nothing more than objects fit to serve a mechanistic purpose.

Being An Intentional Observer

Being an intentional observer often means challenging, or – at the very least – sidestepping most authority figures and structures. In other words, some sources of authority are helpful and meaningful. But authority should always be taken with a grain of salt, and never trusted simply on the grounds of being authority. There should be a valid reason and system for which any authority is in place.

Non-human animal activists would not be able to step into factory farms as formal or even casual observers because there are laws on the books. This is – at least for this book – perhaps the most readily understandable context in which "authority figures" or "laws" are truly just mandates of evil that perpetuate profit and limit freedom of information.

Being an intentional observer means being as respectful as you can be to friends, family and even strangers, but willfully and strategically opposing systems and preferences of violence, injustice and selfishness, no matter how patent or hidden.

Being A Perpetual Observer

Being a perpetual observer is not much different from being an intentional observer. It simply means doing your homework after a discussion, movie, event, activity or meal. Being a perpetual observer is about celebrating those who do good and continuing to serve justice to all.

The Haves And The Have-Nots: The 80-20 Rule

The world is split 80/20: 80 percent of people are the have-nots, 20 percent of people are the haves. 20 percent of people have control over and receive resources, goods and services that 80 percent work to produce. My point is that none of the above excuses apply because millions of people live in incredibly comfortable situations where we have literally infinite choices every day.

Repeating what Paul said in 1 Corinthians: "Looking at it one way, you could say, "Anything goes. Because of God's immense generosity and grace, we don't have to dissect and scrutinize every action to see if it will pass muster." But the point is not to just get by. We want to live well, but our foremost efforts should be to help others live well." - 1 Corinthians 10:23-24□ MSG□

Chapter 3 Thesis:

The need for compassion is everywhere – all places from the lives of the elderly, orphans and homeless non-human animals to the LGBTQ community, individuals from other countries, the disabled and more. Non-human animals and providing them freedom and respect is only one part of a holistically compassionate lifestyle, but it is the most important place to begin, because non-human animals are the most vulnerable group of all the aforementioned with the smallest likelihood of being heard by the average human.

Through affording love, care and respect for non-human animals, we are exponentially more likely to see how all realms of compassion are connected, and become that much more equipped to live a lifestyle of justice.

"But for the sake of some little mouthful of flesh, we deprive a soul of the sun, and light, and of that proportion of life and time they had been born into the world to enjoy." – Plutarch of Chaeronea

Chapter 4: How And Why Christ Calls Christians To Be Exemplary Leaders

"If you love someone who is ruining his or her life because of faulty thinking, and you don't do anything about it because you are afraid of what others might think, it would seem rather than being loving, you are in fact being heartless." – William Wilberforce, English politician, author and abolitionist

Most people don't like to be told that their lifestyle is causing harm. This is one of the main reasons vegans, whether male or female, conflict and experience tension with non-vegans. The typical non-vegan human regards him or herself as a decent human being, especially seeing as they are doing what everyone else is doing. After all, this is how most humans think: "If everyone else is doing it, it can't be that bad or wrong, right?"

And, speaking in a general sense, most people have the capacity to be quite decent, which they often use on a regular basis. Holding the door open for those who cannot do so themselves, helping a friend carry a heavy item, providing local directions to a stranger and covering a shift for a coworker are all commonplace examples of favors that people enact. When executing such favors, most people consider themselves to be acting altruistically or at least helpfully – and they are correct. The issue arises when people stop at this level of thinking and don't consider how they may be able to go above and beyond to live in an even better world.

Most people feel they are fundamentally good people who only occasionally make mistakes. And this can be true enough, at least in a conversational, friendly sense. However, every major movement of the last decade – and even those before that time – were initiated and pushed forward by a minority. Indeed, we usually default to the least amount of effort required unless someone comes along and points out a better way. Naturally, there is a period of cognitive dissonance between recognizing a different option and thinking about it, but before we reach that point, we have to cover a few other fundamentals.

When people are taking any sort of action, they are either minimizing pain or pursuing pleasure. But any action that falls upon this continuum also lands within one of two lenses – people assume the world is either a fundamentally good or evil place. **Or, perhaps better put, the world has the capacity to become worse, or the world has the capacity to become better.**

What an individual's worldview comes down to is the following statement (within every action): either "I can" or "I cannot" do something about problems that I see.

Worldview Fundamentals

Fundamentally, everyone's worldview can be reduced to one of evil or good. Either humans are innately and inherently evil, or we are inherently good. Either we lean towards evil or we lean towards good. Anyone can make the case that certain humans (or even groups) exhibit better behavior than others, but A) this in and of itself is a valuative judgment and B) this glosses over the central point. At the end of the day, everyone thinks the world is a fundamentally, basically good or evil place. Evil roots produce evil people who enact evil behaviors; good roots produce good people who enact good behaviors. So...

Where Does Your Worldview Reveal You To Stand?

Where do you stand? Fundamentally speaking, what is your worldview? Are humans – at their most base level – basically driving evil or fighting against it? Is evil embedded in humans or some other force? Is evil a reality we are all victims of, or is it something we can fight against, weaken and defeat? Once these questions are answered, we find ourselves presented with another set of questions...

What Is The Individual Capable Of?

What is one individual capable of? Great acts, small acts, something in-between? None of the above? All of the above? Is one human capable of creating the same results as another? Is justice replicable? If so, how so? Can it be systematized?

All of these questions, while great to ask in and of themselves, point us to additional elements in the larger picture. Ultimately, since humans are social creatures, we seek to associate and identify with those who share our concepts and ideals. To do otherwise leaves us feeling unaccepted, unappreciated or both. Furthermore, and most essentially (for this chapter), **how we view ourselves is how we view others, and how we view others will invariably become manifest in how we *lead* others – or attempt to.**

Individual Christian Problems To Solve

As we build, approach and implement such mindsets and solutions as a world, however, we Christians have our own battle to solve: the physical health of the church.

Why Do Christians In Particular Have Difficulty With Weight And Health? And What Does This Mean In Relation To Leadership?

In the past, people didn't pay much attention to who was fat and why (at least not within Christian circles). Nowadays, it's quickly becoming no secret that many of the United States' overweight and obese citizens are within Christian churches. The causes of such a phenomenon are still being studied, but there appears to be enough research available to make some accurate conclusions.

From 1986 to 1994, Purdue professor Ken Ferraro collected and analyzed data from over 2,500 people. He was only compiling information from two factors – BMI and religious activity. It's fairly astounding to learn about his findings. Ferraro discovered that religious folks are more often overweight, but he also found disparities between genders. Women were more likely to be overweight or obese if they frequently used religious media such as the radio, TV shows or books. Men were found at lower risk for obesity when they sought out religious services, especially when seeking religion to be comforted.

In 2011, author Matthew Feinstein conducted a study that led to similar results. Across a span of over 2,400 people, he found that 32 percent of the individuals – with the highest religious participation – had the highest chances of becoming obese by middle age. Such results are not encouraging, to say the very least.

So, what lies at the root of such discoveries? Feinstein and Ferraro both pointed out how church or small group gatherings are frequently centered around food

– high calorie, nutrient-deficient food, at that. They also both suggested pastors and executive staff place a higher emphasis on encouraging fellow staff members and the congregation to seek out nutrient-dense foods and fresher food options for church events.

While the "standard American diet" has seen minor fluctuations in what people consider staples, the core of this diet has not changed much. We still love meat, cheese, eggs, all kinds of dairy and enough sugar to cover the surface of the planet. We're smothered in sugar, salt and detrimental fat and we constantly want more of it. We are addicted to these substances and they're ubiquitously offered three times a day, year round.

The advertising we see on television, billboards, the Internet, in grocery stores and everywhere else shows how permeated our minds are in this toxicity. We can't help but feel we want more of it because it's already at our fingertips, just a few dollars away.

So how does this tie into leadership? Well, leaders constantly have the responsibility to do what's best for their people. Leadership is all about leading people to better results through better actions.

Leaders are assigned the job of looking after the most vulnerable and oppressed within their personal groups as well as the globe at large. Leadership is a difficult task in this regard – not because the work is necessarily grueling, but because there are multiple perspectives to keep track of and provide justice for. Justice is inherently an all-inclusive process and requires spreading one's actions wide. It is not enough to ask what the result for the consumer is, or what the end-user's benefit is. The leader must examine the product or service in question all the way from conception to the result, and after-effects.

The natural discipline for a leader to embrace and practice is assessing economic patterns and consumer trends on a *wide* as well as *deep* level. Staying informed of who is oppressed does require keeping up with the news, but more fundamentally and importantly, it requires daily alterations in character. When we go out to the store to buy something, whether for ourselves or others, we have to ask why we're buying it, and if we have options regarding quality or intent. If we are mindlessly stepping through the purchasing experience without examining the roots for integrity, we are missing out on a huge opportunity for justice and causing inadvertent hypocrisy.

Now, do we need to make perfect decisions all the time? No, and in fact, there will be times everyone ends up making decisions in a pinch that result in indirect injustice. The point is to create a system of mindsets and habits worth living off of.

Whenever possible in life, apply the following rule:

More truly can be done with less.

Purchase only what you'll need or use, and only buy more when a tangible circumstance demands it.

More can also be experienced with less. Christian leaders must make the choice to step away from consumerism at all costs.

Yes, it's completely understandable and permissible to purchase enough supplies if you're hosting a party, taking the family on a vacation, going camping or something similar. But this is to miss the point of the big picture and excuse our daily actions, which are far more influential and urgent.

The more important questions to ask often run along these lines:

- How much do I really need for myself?
- Am I trying to sate my dissatisfaction about another area of life with the relentless pursuit of more?
- How much of my stuff do I actually use on a weekly or daily basis?
- Do I always finish the food on my plate?
- Am I always looking for the next trend, gadget, car or home appliance?

Your answers to these questions will determine what kind of work needs to be done in these areas. Contingent upon your results of course, keep in mind to commit to action rather than just words or loose ideas of the person you may want to be one day.

Christ's Emphasis On Love And Compassion

It is well known that Christ is most famous for His embodiment of love towards all. Some would challenge this prospect, but a quick and truthful examination of His daily actions reveal nothing else.

Christ was unabashedly known for his associations with the "fringe crowd." Tax collectors, addicts, prostitutes – the outcasts. In fact, the single group most known for opposing Christ was the Pharisees, a subset of Jews who often openly flaunted their "righteousness" in front of others, hoping to win points with God.

Christ was an advocate of the down-and-outs, women, children, the elderly, the sick, poor, lame, deaf, blind and many more. He paid attention to those who most other people simply sidestepped. His love was bold, and perfect, for that matter. He hadn't an ounce of interest in pleasing people; only offering true love and truth in the most graceful way possible.

Ever since then, those who profess to be Christians have made human attempts to imitate Christ. According to the Christian worldview, one receives eternal salvation only through faith in Christ's blood sacrifice. No human is perfect while on Earth, and this is readily manifest around us. I will be the first to admit I'm not perfect, and I'll certainly never be while on Earth. Honest Christians attempt to do the most good they can in honor of the Lord and for the good of humans, but we all fall short, and it can get quite messy at times.

At this point in the book, there's no question that Christ is the archetypal example of all things good: love, justice, grace, truth, mercy, kindness, compassion, strength and joy. The bigger (and sometimes only) question that remains is: "How do those who profess to imitate Christ imitate Him to the truest and fullest ability possible?"

Christ came to heal the sick, not to help those who already think they've got everything together. In other words, Christ lived on Earth to help people who needed and wanted help – not to try to correct those who thought they already knew everything or always chose the "right answers." We must do the same by speaking to all, but particularly to those whose ears are sensitive to our message.

Christ's Emphasis On Sacrifice

Being sent to Earth as fully God and fully man, Christ was in an entirely unique position. He was also on the Earth only 33 years before His body and spirit were used as the ultimate sacrifice for all of mankind's sin.

During His ministry, He lived without a home or bed, and often only received food when others were able to provide it. He was up-front with His disciples about this before they ever truly set foot upon the journey with Him. Their journey was of a vagabond nature, preaching the truth and helping others as they traveled around, but never really having "roots" – a place to lay one's head.

To say the very least, Christ was acquainted with sacrifice. Forgoing physical comforts was one thing, but living out a (shorter) life for the sole purpose of being sacrificed on a cross was a whole different level.

Even on a basic level, we have so much to learn from this picture. For one, it's painfully clear that Jesus and His disciples owned few or zero possessions. They were constantly at the mercy (or lack thereof) of those around them and often had to make do with very little. This forced them from the beginning to kill any materialism they had in their hearts.

What does this reveal? It shows us that material

possessions often stand in direct contrast to one's purpose in life. Just having a bunch of "things" often causes trouble, if for no reason other than to distract one from the bigger picture of daily life.

Indeed, in Luke 18 we see Christ speaking with a materially wealthy man who was wondering what he needed to do for eternal life. Christ instructed him to give away his material possessions to the poor, and to then follow Him. The man didn't want to hear this; it's probably the last statement he wanted to hear.

What does this story mean for us? We can take the principle behind this story and apply it to our individual lives. There is usually at least one thing in our life we don't want to give up. Sometimes, it is the very person, object, pastime or fixation that is preventing us from deeper relationships, more whole living and a closer connection to God.

Also, there are oftentimes multiple things we all don't like giving up. The list can include, but not be limited to: money, energy, our thought life, consistency of action and our comfort zone with most areas of life. Through gentle but persistent nudges of the Spirit, Christ calls us to leave our material and Earthly comforts behind in pursuit of love and justice, and to lean on Him for guidance when the next step isn't as clear as we'd like it to be.

Paying Attention To The World Around Us

When you're young, in most ways you're at the mercy of and reliant upon the support of your parents. Life is generally good. You get free food, baths and tons of time to sleep and play. You're making friendships, gradually meeting new people, making memories and doing other things children do. It's typically a beautiful sight for family members and passerby alike.

As you grow older, responsibilities mount, and so do the darker sides of life. You begin to recognize that you're not perfect, and nothing is brought on a silver platter. As M. Scott Peck famously said, life becomes (and is) difficult.

There's no more silver lining to every single day, and there is heartbreak, monotony, frustration, loneliness and abandon. These things hurt, and understandably so. In response, many of us try to restore the images and feelings of life we experienced when younger. It's seen as only natural to do so; who doesn't want to live an enjoyable, pain-free life?

Life becomes more difficult as you grow older because truth enters in. There's less to shield oneself with, and consequently, there are fewer (if any) excuses via which one's actions can be dismissed.

Individuals garner increasing responsibilities as they transition from children to adults because adults are nearly universally seen as possessing greater and longer-lasting ability. In other words, to whom is given greater ability, equally great output and results are expected.

Adults do often enjoy more fruits of their labor than children, because adults engage in a world in which there is more responsibility, but greater freedom. Strangely, however, as many of us transition to adults (in the formal sense of the word), we often lose our childlike curiosity that drove much of our learning in early years.

Children are known for how many questions they ask, and perhaps more importantly, how many layers of questions they engage in. For example, a child may ask, "Why are there laces on the shoes?" A parent can respond by saying something such as laces help to keep a shoe secure on the foot. The child may respond with, "Why do shoes need to stay on your foot?" And the parent might say, "Because we can trip if the shoe doesn't stay in place."

This is a lighthearted and simplified example of a round of questions, but the principle remains the same: A child is unafraid to ask numerous, multi-tiered questions around one topic, whereas an adult may often refrain from deeper conversation (depending on the topic).

It's a strange (and sad) state of events with most adults, however, because we often love to know about meaningless things and categorically avoid those most pressing and urgent of matters. Wholeheartedly investigating the truth of a premise necessitates the ensuing personal responsibility within said premise, which means most people don't want to look at the truth in the first place.

To put it another way, many adults avoid observing the world around us because through logic, it calls for being involved and taking responsibility for our actions. We can no longer stand around as children, waiting for those we trust to change the course of action, hoping that wishful thinking will wipe the deep blood stains of injustice away.

None of this is to say there aren't good people in the world, whether Christian or otherwise. Well-intentioned and consistently-behaving people exist everywhere. It's easy to find people recycling plastic and paper (especially in urban areas), carpooling to work, taking shorter showers and even trying to lessen consumerist spending in general.

When asked, many adults express concern for environmental preservation, ending mass causes of pollution and maintaining our Earth well enough for future generations to survive on it. All of these answers and data indicate that just about everyone desires to take care of the Earth and those who live in it. Yet bring up vegetarianism or veganism as a way to solve many (if not all) of the world's ills, and chances are you'll receive quizzical looks at best and incendiary insults at worst.

In his book *For Love Of Animals,* Fordham University professor Charles Camosy thoroughly presents the concept of Christian justice. He illustrates that the authentic Christian is called to a fully integral, holistic approach to justice – leaving no stone unturned, in other words. Camosy also drives home the point that the Christian should be particularly skeptical and critical of any systems or structures that promote consumerism, violence and autonomy.

Further, Camosy's points and musings – when applied to common, real-life scenarios – are indeed true. It's all too common to see a group of Christians gathering to discuss their latest mission trip effort, a prison/orphanage visit or something of the like, all while enjoying a meal of chicken sandwiches, fish tacos or hotdogs.

When reading the above paragraph, most people would hardly bat an eye. In fact, most people would probably start getting a tad hungry based on the mention of food. Speciesism flies almost entirely under the radar for most people, simply because corporate interests and cultural conditioning have succeeded in convincing the world's majority of a potent lie.

The Importance Of Making Small Changes And Doing Them Now

This section is primarily focused at any Christians reading this book. Fellow Christians: Frankly, if we are to be authentically committed to doing good in the world and doing as much as we can, we cannot afford to only work with other Christians. Here's what I mean.

Our world is too messed up to be selective about who we do good things with. Christians are only one fraction of the world, and if there are good actions that more than just Christians want to take, we should be teaming up with them. Incidentally, this is where most problems crop up, because a lot of people only feel comfortable taking major actions with those we feel comfortable with.

But this is also the crossroads at which larger questions also crop up: What exactly are we afraid of? What makes us uncomfortable? Are we as Christians insecure about our own faith, which is what makes us hesitant about interacting with those of other faiths?

These are challenging questions to ask and even more

challenging to answer, for the most part. Yet, every honest Christian must acknowledge them; otherwise, we run into the danger of our faith being practically non-existent in our regular lives.

Take the following for example. Whether you are a student, working full-time, raising a family, retired or virtually anything in between, you are going to come in contact with individuals who have different beliefs than you. It's really this simple. No one truly lives in a vacuum; otherwise you can make the argument you aren't living at all. Being removed from all other forms and walks of life is essentially being in prison (whether literal or metaphorical).

The world is currently 7.5 billion people, and most of us live in an area where we're in contact with at least two cultural faiths or cultural lifestyles. This is to say that straights come in contact with gays, atheists come in contact with Christians and vegans come in contact with carnists. Everyone is slightly different from another and this is (in a better world) what can make life so interesting.

Here's where the rubber hits the road, however. You can profess to be a Christian in your private life, but if your beliefs do not manifest into actions within your public life, are you really still a Christian? If you read your Bible at home, but when out at a party on Friday night, you're hanging with a few Muslim and atheist friends and you avoid mentioning your own faith out of fear of potentially causing them grief, is your Christian faith legitimate?

To be fair, most of the atheists, Muslims and followers of other faiths I know would not take offense at the mention of the Christian faith within a friend, especially not a close friend. It often takes significantly more effort to piss someone off. Yet, the point remains: At what point does the typical Christian feel comfortable – or uncomfortable – about even mentioning their faith?

Here's another analogy to provide support. Suppose you're a married man or woman (if you aren't already married). You spend time with your spouse at home – making meals, enjoying down time, conversing about life, and even making love. It's a joyful time on most days, and you often imagine you couldn't be happier while at home. It reaches the point where you're so enthralled with your spouse that you love him or her, but since you're both in the house so often, people often don't get the chance to become familiar with your spouse.

So, when you leave and go outside, it's difficult to be vocal about him or her, since they aren't out in the real world to begin with. People may be confused at best and offended at worst when you try to bring up the subject on rare occasions only. "What do you mean you're married? I've never seen your spouse outside before. Are you sure you aren't just pulling my leg?" they may remark. And their questions and concerns are generally justified. If your private life doesn't match your public life with as much integrity as you can muster, there's cause for legitimate concern.

In order to maximize the potential of making small changes and doing them now, we can lean on the wisdom of investor and author James Altucher's "one percent rule." The one percent rule simply states:

when viewing all vital areas of your life (relationships, finances, work, health, spirituality, values), practice becoming better by one percent every day.

In other words, there's no need to improve by leaps and bounds every day. This is both unrealistic and too time-consuming; not everyone has four free hours per day to drastically improve a skill. Instead, simply focus on one small aspect you can improve by one percent on each day, in every major area of your life. Skip buying dessert after a meal; tell someone how you're grateful for them; pour a bit more effort into your work project; so on and so forth. Before you know it, after a year has gone by, you'll be 100 percent more skilled in an area, or greater!

The Urgency Needed For Our World, And For Making A Difference

Christians are called to make a difference every day, wherever they are. This is a massive task – certainly one that cannot be undertaken alone. Despite this, so often, we Christians attempt to do our difference-making within our own circles, or within our comfort zone at the very least. This often leads to little or no results, disappointment and lack of recurring motivation.

Too often, we're trying to make a difference without doing anything *differently*. This is not to dissuade people from taking any kind of action and actually moving a goal forward, but we must analyze our motives – and methods – if we're really going to ignite lasting change.

As Christians, we should not be afraid to challenge the beliefs of the secular. We should not be afraid of calling the truth out into the open. If and when we challenge the norms of our world, those who are legitimate will stand back up. Yes; we must present the truth in love, but we also must uphold the truth everywhere we go. Otherwise, our love is actually hypocrisy.

Change Is Staring Us Right In The Face

We live in a time that is both more capable and more sin-ravaged than any other time in the world. Wars still rage, brothels still profit and souls are still tortured. The need for change is staring us – as humans and especially as Christians – right back in the face. We either stand for something or we die for nothing.

What Do We Want To Be Known By?

As Christians, we have a daily challenge of deciding what to be known by. Every action we take is either one that illuminates who Christ is, or one that clouds Him. There's no such thing as being an "average" Christian, per se. We're either moving the Kingdom forward, or holding it back.

Every day, we have the opportunity to align our actions with our values and beliefs as closely as possible. Most Christians (myself included, at one point) simply want to go to church, work their jobs, spend time with their families and enjoy outings with their friends. Are any of these things inherently wrong? No. But if we really take the time to examine what living the Christian life means, as we have done in this book, we are faced with the fact that (unfortunately) more often, we have to press against the influences of secular culture rather than simply work "inside" them.

Some may say that the work and advancements I'm describing in this book are reserved for the most tenacious and ambitious of us. But if we look at how Christianity itself began, we see this isn't true at all. Christianity began (in many ways) as Christ enlisting His disciples to follow Him – which, by the way, were young folks. In other words, Christianity (from a movement perspective) started via a small group of committed individuals who were willing to go against the grain of the culture around them. They worked *in* the world but not *for* the world, or *because* of the world. They sought to raise everyone's attention to the Creator of the Universe, and the only Being who could save them from sin.

All of this comes back to one question: Do we want to be known by our decision to remain in personal comfort at the sacrifice of others' freedom, or our conviction and commitment to fighting for holistic, lasting justice?

"I would unite with anybody to do right and nobody to do wrong." – Frederick Douglass

Chapter 4 Thesis:

As Christians, we have a responsibility to get our own act together before we aim to convince anyone else of the merits of veganism or justice as a whole. Christ calls His followers to be holistically and consummately prepared for the journey ahead – being committed in mind, heart and *body,* not just one or two of the three.

We can be the timid bystanders upon the edge of the desperate need for world change, or we can be the very catalysts and juggernauts of justice that make a lasting impact on all those we touch. The world is also watching us, waiting to see if we will crumble entirely or grow stronger with every step.

"Kindness and compassion towards all living beings is a mark of a civilized society. Racism, economic deprival, dog fighting and cock fighting, bullfighting and rodeos are all cut from the same defective fabric: violence. Only when we have become nonviolent towards all life will we have learned to live well ourselves." – Cesar Chavez

Chapter 5: Non-Human Animal Abuse And The Christian Responsibility

"I would go to the deeps a hundred times to cheer a downcast spirit. It is good for me to have been afflicted, that I might know how to speak a word in season to one that is weary." – Charles Spurgeon

How Animal Abuse Is Swept Under The Rug Across The World

One of the arguments thrown against veganism is that if we *can* use non-human animals as food, we might as well. Unfortunately, this argument does not hold up to logical scrutiny. The idea that you can take advantage of a creature simply via your raw ability is called the "might makes right" argument. This is how bullies think. They think that since they *can* beat up another kid on the playground, they *should,* and often do. But clearly, no one comes to the rescue of the bully here. They come to the rescue of the innocent child with a bloody face.

It is clear there is a problem when someone who is stronger or more physically dominant becomes aggressive towards an innocent individual. We do not praise the oppressor for his strength or ambition; we scream out to protect the oppressed and highlight the fact that injustice has taken place. Nothing is different when comparing bullies on a playground or rapists in a trafficking ring to consumers in the landscape of non-human animal agriculture. **The exact actions may be different, but the nature of them all is the same: oppression, violence and injustice.** Excessive violence, blatant torture, invariable enslavement and imminent death are all necessary parts of turning non-human animals into food. We persist with this framework (out of sight and out of mind) because it is the only series of actions that is able to produce enough non-human animals' dead bodies at the global rate of demand.

Naturally, vegans do not subscribe to might-makes-right because we hold that sentient life is inherently valuable, simply because it exists. We do not need to take advantage of other forms of sentient life for any reason. This is not about merely sounding like a better person – it is about being transparent about how we line up our diets with the rest of the innate logic that exists plainly in our day-to-day lives.

What Do Consumers Do About The Problem Of "Out Of Sight, Out Of Mind?"

In the countries that have the highest meat consumption, which are often the most densely populated countries, we face a gravely humiliating dilemma. We love the sight, scent and taste of various meats, and we often fantasize about how to create new meat-centric recipes, but we can't stand the sight or sound of factory farm videos.

To be clear again, it's not the average consumer's fault that such videos are heavily repressed by the powers of the animal agriculture industry. There are already dozens of laws on the books that prevent individuals from taking footage of slaughterhouse procedures, or even getting close to any of them.

This is all simply because the more people know the truth about what's required to produce non-human animals as commodities by the billions, demand would drop much faster than it already is. I'm positive many executive staffers and CEOs within the animal ag industry hate the reality of killing non-human animals themselves. Thousands of people simply want to make a buck and get it done however they want.

Most vegans often share images that speak on the following: "If it's not good enough for your eyes, why is it good enough for your mouth?" This statement harps on the disconnect between how meat is a favored dish nearly worldwide, yet no one wants to see non-human animals undergoing unnecessary pain and suffering. Melanie Joy speaks at length about this non-human animal harm/taste bud pleasure disconnect in her book, *Why We Love Dogs, Eat Pigs And Wear Cows.*

Since humans don't regularly seek out challenging, contrary information as is (due to inborn drives to maximize pleasure and avoid pain), most full-time vegans alive today (especially those from developed countries) were first confronted with reality by someone else who had gone vegan before them. It takes courage to look at what you don't want to see. But it causes a bigger problem to evade what you know is true, even when it makes you uncomfortable.

How Christ Followers Can Set A Wonderful New Example

The world is ***desperate*** for **fresh infusions of legitimate, Christlike love.** It's no secret that the world at large is not fond of Christians right now, especially American Christians. Leave it to books like *unChristian* by David Kinnaman and *Culture Shock* by Chip Ingram to illustrate how deeply entrenched and emotionally incendiary important issues have become.

The world is also looking for capable, strong, loving people to solve pressing problems. Christians can be those people. No one is perfect, but the world (and other Christians) rightly hold us to the standard of high excellence. If we want to be perceived as legitimate in the eyes of the world, we must be both competent and welcoming. We cannot effectively convey the message of Christ with only one of these traits.

The Importance Of Embodying Peace And Not Allowing Violence To Reign

Throughout the typical day of many folks living in developed countries, it's mostly easy to avoid violence while getting to work, spending time with family at home or enjoying a night out with friends. Violence is frequently associated with crime and drug-related offenses. However, the fullest picture involves much more than these sometimes "Hollywood-esque" mental pictures of wrongdoing.

Violence as a concept and reality is often looked down upon. Indeed, most of our world deems it an unacceptable activity on moral grounds alone. It poses a dilemma, then, that many of our media choices and recreational activities contain "properly packaged" violence.

Wrestling, boxing, bullfighting and UFC matches are routine choices for entertainment, especially among men. Another stereotypical choice in recreation comes in the form of grilling, which is the celebration and aggrandization of a non-human animal's flesh being prepared as a meal.

We shun violence when it appears too personal or unjustified, yet we accept it and even celebrate the products of it when it serves our own interests or needs.

126

What we often fail to ask ourselves is what the purpose of violence is at all:

- What ends does violence serve?

_____

_____

_____

_____

- What "societal gap" is violence filling? What problem is it solving?

_____

_____

_____

_____

- Why is violence chosen over other alternatives?

_____

_____

_____

- Why is violence so satisfactory?

- What is entertainment violence doing that something else cannot?

What we see in many dogfighting and cockfighting rings (and other similar entertainment choices) is the viewers get a rise out of seeing two or more non-human animals tear each other apart. It's some kind of twisted satisfaction onlookers receive from conflict at its very core: the manifestation of physical violence.

We find that when we seek out a form of carnal release or satisfaction, it is because we are unable to find satisfaction in other components of our character or daily lives. Violence becomes satisfactory when something else in our life is missing, or impaired. When what is best is beyond the reach of our comfort zone, requires donning a separate perspective or requires our actions to be consistent with our values, we frequently settle for inferior solutions or tastes.

So much of the "entertainment violence" available in movies, video games, TV shows and live performances is tied to consumerism. Violence often goads further violence, because where a small amount elicits a reaction from humans, a larger amount can bring about more.

When consumerism is the dominant cultural influence (especially a factor within food preferences), it becomes more challenging and less comfortable to break that cycle.

Every Day You Have A Choice To Live Your Beliefs

At the end of each day, all we can do is look back and see if our actions reflected our beliefs. Oftentimes this is easier said than done. Fortunately, if we take a few minutes to periodically check if our actions are performing well, we don't have to put as much effort into thinking about the right thing to do in the first place:

- What are my beliefs?

_____

_____

_____

_____

- What is the core my beliefs stand on?

_____

_____

_____

_____

- What are my beliefs about food?

_____

_____

_____

_____

- What are the most influential books, movies, people or organizations that have altered my thoughts about food?

_____

_____

- Has anything caused me conflict about food? Has it involved a person?

Wait A Minute Brad, Do Non-Human Animals Matter More Than Humans?

All this talk of valuing non-human animals and protecting them from harm may have you wondering, "Is Brad trying to convince me that I only matter as much as a pig or cow, but not more?" This is a valid question, but fear not – equally valid answers lie ahead.

Granted, it seems challenging for most Christians to see non-human animals as valuable in their own right. Through talk of veganism and appreciating non-human animals for their inherent worth, perspectives may change if facts are presented in a respectable light and people are given a chance to ask their questions, without concern of bullying or misanthropic commentary.

For the record, we must clear the air as much as possible. I am not (and likely never will be) an advocate for schools for pigs, automobiles for cows, libraries for chickens or anything of the sort. Non-human animals are valuable without needing (or even wanting) the same institutions and material possessions as humans.

I don't think I need to go into detail for you to understand what I mean. While of course I see innate value in non-human animals simply for existing, I am not equating and will not try to equate the rights or freedoms of non-humans with humans. The problem exists when humans think that non-human animals deserve of nothing in their own right, simply for existing. Even worse, it appears some corners of humanity think non-humans are deserving of nothing more than torture and death, simply because they are not human.

This is a problem of perspective. Every pet owner would defend his or her beloved non-human animal from ill fate or demise, across a spectrum of "normalcy" all the way to ruthlessness. In other words, of course dog and cat lovers defend their pets against death. But to love dogs and cats and leave commodified non-human animals in the pits is an arbitrary decision that necessitates violence, cruelty and systematic injustice.

Many humans trying to confound veganism present the "dog and human drowning situation." This is a theoretical (rarely real) scenario where a dog and human are drowning side by side. If given the chance to save only one, who would you save?

This "argument" is a frequent copout for those trying to persuade others that *humans* matter to the necessary exclusion that non-human animals have *little or no value.*

In other words, this hypothetical instance is a lose-lose situation. No matter which option you pick, a life is going to be lost. If you save the human, an innocent dog drowns in an ugly death. If you save the dog, a (potentially) innocent human also meets their ugly demise.

The most practical and realistic question to ask is:

"What do you do on a regular basis?"

How do you protect both humans and non-human animals with your daily lifestyle choices? Going vegan is the ultimate solution and non-harmful/non-partisan choice for living in and creating a world where *everyone* thrives and is valuable.

The dog/human drowning scenario is one that conveniently ignores the fact that 150+ billion land and sea creatures are killed annually just to supply greedy human demand for products we don't need. If we conveniently allow for factory farming, it seems we have our priorities completely botched.

It's not that non-human animals matter more than humans; it's that they don't matter *less* than humans. The fact that we're treating non-human animals like they matter less or matter zero is why we have so many problems in our world.

"As Long As There Are Slaughterhouses, There Will Be Battlefields"

Violence, just like other forces enacted at the hands of humans, must stop at the most fundamental of levels, otherwise it will only continue. This may seem counterintuitive, but at a closer glance, we see how effective it is.

Non-human animals have been utilized in agriculture and as food for thousands of years; many experts estimate this form of their oppression began 10,000-12,000 years ago.

All movements of justice have involved an oppressor and the oppressed; one with a voice, and one without. What virtually all non-human animals have in common is that at some point, humans have oppressed them.

We take sea creatures and lock them up in aquariums; we take land animals and place them in cages; we capture birds of the air and entrap them in rooms. All of these are patently unnatural forms of existence for these creatures. We keep them captive in the name of "science, experimentation, and entertainment." We see no problem with taking droves of creatures and forcing them to do our will, but we create (and further incite) madness and uproar when one perceivably "innocent" creature is cast down by ill fate and met with an untimely death.

Thus is the sinister victory of slaughterhouses. The only method through which the animal agriculture industry is able to sustain itself year after year is through scrupulous concealment. Keeping their bloodshed beyond your eyes, away from your ears and out of your mind is the product of hundreds of hours of planning and strategy. This takes a notable amount of effort, but it is the solitary stroke they need. As long as the murders are disconnected from the supermarket and the family dinner table, whole clusters of society will continue to purchase what they're all too familiar with, and often thank God for such a "blessing."

Only when the smallest, youngest and most innocent creature is pardoned from deplorable horrors and given the free, happy life he or she deserves will the injustice cease forever. The utter lunacy that is every form of injustice must be ruthlessly examined at its core: for what reason can any unnecessary atrocity be committed? **Alas, the time for such a simple question is rarely even found, because it is almost never searched for.**

Allow an individual in power to create a selfish motive, rally others around their initiative and create personal motivation for the new individuals involved, and you may have an unstoppable force. Thus was (at least loosely) the case with Hitler and his minions. They were trying to carry out the mission he had convinced them was "right." Unless small groups of tireless, dedicated truth-seekers persist in the war against falsehood and injustice, tyranny and oppression – in all its manifestations – can take control anywhere.

Good, everyday citizens must have the courage to examine the inner workings of their daily lives and the deepest postures of their hearts and minds. Only through such steadfast and transparent exercises can people like you, reader of this book, discover why and how to truly live a virtuous, just life.

If you see a video on the Internet that makes you cringe in shame or freeze in horror, there's a precise reason for your emotions in that moment. The person who recommended the video to you is not pulling black-hat marketing tactics on you; you're simply experiencing a human reaction through which your conscience is saying, "Something's not right here. I need to figure out which side of the fence I land on."

Too often, we experience friction between feeling in our gut that something is wrong, and trying to justify our existing behavior in our mind. The technical term for this phenomenon is called cognitive dissonance (if you want to read more about this term and other social phenomena that frequently surround it, I highly recommend researching it).

The point is that if you feel something is wrong deep down in your gut, it probably is. It can be likened to the same feeling you get when a deer runs right in front of your car on a dimly lit road or when another car veers out of lane and almost crashes into you. Both situations were close calls, and you instinctively knew something was wrong. You have to do something about it, if you can (which with veganism, you can), and learn from the personal experience you had. Your individual choices and voice have far more influence than you probably believe.

It can seem like going vegan won't end wars overseas overnight – and the truth is, it won't. But it doesn't mean your actions won't have a ripple effect. In fact, they will! Your actions will cause your new beliefs to become stronger and more lucid, which in turn will strengthen your actions. Intentionally "voting violence out" through your daily actions will provide a lens through which you continually see other choices in life the same way.

This in turn will cause others to consider the same, or at the very least, decide they aren't on the same page (whether consciously or subconsciously). All of this together, observed and enacted over a long enough period of time, can create a vegan (therefore, ahimsa) world.

Opposing All Unnecessary Violence And Being Good

When God was issuing the Israelites towards battle, He was utilizing their human forces to wipe out a city, village or entity that was a grave offender towards God. At other times, due to the unfaith of the Israelites and their betrayal towards God, God sometimes used wartime and the absence of peace to punish His own people.

In other words, the virtual entirety of violence from human to human in the Old Testament was between a group receiving justice and one serving justice (or people receiving justice amongst themselves). Evil communities or individuals were getting what they deserved; justice was being delivered.

Non-human animal violence is a completely different story. Since they are defenseless against the powers and schemes of humans, a fresh set of moral rules come into play. If you do not take the side of the oppressed, you are *necessarily* taking the side of the oppressor. Please understand I do not say this to belittle or demean; however, the facts are the facts.

When topics such as this are read about or discussed in person, people often hear such statements as pointed accusations, which is understandable from an emotional vantage point. However, there is more to the picture and we must view each element logically.

As a global culture and certainly in the United States, we often get wrapped up in aiming to be "good people." Despite some disagreement about what is good or even best, most humans agree being a good person is something to strive for. Most humans also agree that being a good person is something people should do consistently, not just when we feel like it. I would love to dive into the details of what really comprises a "good" person, but for the sake of brevity within this book, we must discuss what "being good" means and looks like within the context of veganism.

Being good is about more than simply thinking you're good. Anyone can go about their day as usual, thinking they're being good or even having a good day, and call it all "good." But unless we have at least some kind of minimal framework with which to compare different types of goodness, we are only fooling ourselves.

For example, most mothers and fathers want to be able to provide for their children, which regularly includes having meals ready when needed. To the typical American family, a selection of meat as the main course with perhaps a grain and/or some vegetables on the side may be tonight's dinner.

If an individual is not looking deeper, this may all sound normal and hardly worth batting an eye. It's considered a good action to provide food for a hungry family, and most people close the door right there. For the record, it is in fact a great thing to fix a meal for those in need of nourishment! But if we all want the world we profess to dream of, we must continually observe the differences between reality and the dream world, and accordingly edit our actions until we live our values.

If we do look deeper, we discover that there are numerous ways the aforementioned meal can be made better. Stating that one thing is good and another is better directly implies that one set of actions is "acceptable" but another is *optimal*.

For a vegan to challenge a meat eater's actions or ethics is often hot-button ground. Even a vegan being in the room who has not yet said much about their convictions can be enough for a behavioral omnivore to poke fun at the vegan for their thoughts.

People understand the implied statement is if someone is not consuming non-human animal products, there must be a reason why. Usually when an individual abstains from a certain option that the majority deem acceptable, people also understand the abstinent individual must perceive said option to be wrong, somehow.

In the instance of recreational drugs, many folks – even some users themselves – understand substance abuse to be morally (or at least socially) undesirable. Thousands of scientific documents throughout the world exist on the detrimental effects of substance abuse. Tobacco and alcohol abuse alone have wreaked havoc that few other substances have. For something that is more readily taboo by the public, individuals understand why someone would abstain from said substances.

In the instance of chicken nuggets, hot dogs, macaroni and cheese or even milkshakes – all of which are regular purchases that accrue millions of dollars annually – the response you'll get for abstaining here is guaranteed to be mixed at best. I've personally encountered probably every reaction in the book in five years alone.

Some friends and family have responded by commending me for my choices and sharing more of their own thoughts on the subject. Occasionally they'll ask me what I think about a particular food or food group. One of the more common questions I've received is whether or not fish are included in a vegan's diet. It is hard not to immediately laugh this one off.

At other times, people have been less agreeable. I've had many folks "joke" with me about how great meat tastes, how the non-human animals provide such wonderful tasting food and similar statements. I often respond by letting people know if they're interested in diving into a full-fledged discussion where both people get to express their thoughts, I'm happy to do so. Otherwise, I tell people I'm not open to conversation. This often causes the other speaker to sober up to a considerable degree and cease their discourse.

The truth is, vegans *do* want to discuss ethics of food with omnivores, meat lovers, paleo enthusiasts and everyone in-between. But the vast majority of us desire to do so with a setting and time frame in which both people can effectively field their questions and seek responses. Naturally, all individuals desire this, but too often people are caught in the middle of situations with limited time and a context in which another activity is happening. I cannot tell you how many times I've been asked "Don't you miss XYZ product?" only to have to respond with a hasty and somewhat deficient answer, merely to fulfill the question asker's intent.

At the end of the day, your actions speak more than your words. Truly, your actions are the only components that speak in the first place. Words are merely speculation – placeholders, if you will. Conversations are how emotional and mental evaluations take place, but actions are when theory and speculation are actually put into practice. This is why someone who wants to make a career change can really only be deemed an individual of their word when specific actions have been accomplished.

Returning to our example of the American family, in order to objectively know what's good, we must scrutinize the available facts and critically examine what our actions look like in light of said facts. What's considered good by one person might only be the tip of the iceberg in terms of true potential.

Before we arrive at this section's thesis, we must acknowledge another reality of society. We cannot rely on larger society to decide what's good or even best in the long run. This is proven by the fact that most people engage in the bare minimum necessary to live a satisfactory life.

We see evidence of this fact in most corporate contexts. The lowest level of performance a business is willing to tolerate will be the highest benchmark most people reach for. In other words, employees are relatively quick to notice what's acceptable and what's not, and from that point people recognize where they want to land. Intrinsic motivation is the most powerful impetus for most people, and unless people have this, few will rise to higher levels of performance without being prodded.

This same concept applies to life in a big-picture sense. Via our family members, friends and others we choose to surround ourselves with, we slowly (or quickly) decide what we deem acceptable. When facing contrary forces of any kind, cognitive dissonance sets in and we may briefly wonder which side of a topic or argument is correct. Unless we choose to apply greater diligence to our current mode of thought, we may remain stuck in the ways we've conditioned for ourselves via our surroundings.

People are against animal cruelty, almost as a rule. All facets of the animal agriculture industry understand this. Therefore, in order to profit or even stay in business, they must forcibly remove the barbarous realities of their industry from the public eye. Otherwise, people begin noticing the savagery behind the veil, and – naturally – begin questioning it.

Despite hundreds of attempts year-round from non-human animal activists to bring the truth to light, animal industry lobbyists, lawyers and business owners themselves fight back just as severely. It's a treacherous battle – the results of which will one day reveal which fork in the road humanity has chosen to tread.

Is Veganism Really The Most Important Ethical Foundation?

If you had the power every single day to reduce and help eliminate the single most powerful source of the world's most widespread suffering, would you act on that power? I can only imagine everyone who understands the implications of it would.

Before you harp on the idea that there are other, more important problems happening in the world, please allow me to elaborate on this point.

A lot of people claim humanitarian issues and wars are the bigger problems happening right now. But what do the roots of these problems consist of? Wars and humanitarian injustices consist of gross exploitation of innocent or neutral things. In other words, the reason humans are treated poorly is because non-human animals – fellow living beings that are just as valid as humans – have been exploited far longer.

The Lord's Resistance Army (LRA) exists because Joseph Kony and his associates were insane and depraved yet smart enough to know how to round up children and get them to kill their own families. The same is done with non-human animals every single day (in the sense that we round them up and grossly abuse/kill them), because they're at the mercy of our actions and choices. They have no choice but to do what we force them to do, simply because we're utilizing them for our own profit and selfish pleasure.

Wars often begin as battles over who will get access to certain resources. If animal agriculture and the animal exploitation industry at large is rapidly removing most of the resources we know and need, doesn't it make alarmingly loud and perfect sense that we stop the mindless waste of resources that simply stokes our non-human animal-centric taste buds and wallets? There's no other solution for all the world's ills that can be so rapidly and readily implemented.

Christians Were Actually The First To Lead The Charge With Veganism

In addition to the quotes I already placed throughout this book, I have a few quotes below on vegetarianism and veganism from distinctly Christian thinkers, writers and orators:

"If to be feelingly alive to the sufferings of my fellow-creatures is to be a fanatic, I am one of the most incurable fanatics ever permitted to be at large."

– William Wilberforce, widely considered the first major anti-slavery and anti-animal cruelty Christian activist of the modern world

---

"By killing, man suppresses in himself, unnecessarily, the highest spiritual capacity, that of sympathy and pity towards living creatures like himself and by violating his own feelings becomes cruel."

– Leo Tolstoy, philosopher, novelist and considered one of the greatest writers of all time

---

"I believe in my heart that faith in Jesus Christ can and will lead us beyond an exclusive concern for the well-being of other human beings to the broader concern for the well-being of the birds in our backyards, the fish in our rivers, and every living creature on the face of the earth."

– John Wesley, *God's Covenant with Animals*

When people make judgment calls on how to proceed with their own actions, they like to know what they are doing is right. And, at the very least, people like to know what they're doing is making a difference.

This is one reason people get hung up on veganism. They begin to see the problem as so large and as though there's no hope for solving the problem in time. In truth, the time that remains for humanity on Earth may not be enough to reverse the afflictions we've brought upon our fellow Earth-dwellers and ourselves. However, this does not remove us from responsibility of doing what we can do while we still have time, energy and freedom to do it. The more momentum we have, the better results we'll see.

As Christians, we follow God because we hold Him as the ultimate standard of goodness and truth. While being vegetarian or vegan is not a prerequisite to Christianity, God speaks in no vague terms that He derives no joy or happiness from the exploitation or sacrifice of non-human animals. Indeed, this reality plus all the information we have available about the

145

world we currently live in shows us God is honored when we respect and uphold His creation, take only what we need in terms of food and protect the creatures He lovingly crafted (ourselves included) with bold, decisive systems of justice, truth and love.

Since all humans are biased, we are faced with constantly seeking and reiterating what it means to follow God in the best way. In other words, even as Christians among Christians, we will occasionally disagree about what the right thing is to do. This does not pose a problem as long as we all live and work with each other in love. We simply have to afford as ruthless an analysis of the truth as we are deep and compassionate in love.

Chapter 5 Thesis:

Non-human animal abuse is both more widespread and more effectively covered up than we realize. Violence against non-human animals extends beyond the dogfighting villains and fur coat manufacturers we see on TV and in Internet petitions; it's the very force producing chicken flesh, cow parts and hen menstrual cycles for the daily meals we take for granted.

Christians must not only be committed to stopping patently public forms of injustice, we must be committed to seeking out, exposing and combating the evils of hidden injustice as well. Christ expects nothing less of us, as He commands us in Isaiah 1:17 to "Say no to wrong. Learn to do good. Work for justice. Help the down-and-out. Stand up for the homeless. Go to bat for the defenseless."

"We ought to oppose evil by every righteous means in our power, but not by evil." – Leo Tolstoy

Chapter 6: Creating Dynamic Systems For Justice

"If a man is not making a pretense of work, but is working in order to accomplish the matter he has in hand, his actions will necessarily follow one another in a certain sequence determined by the nature of the work. If he postpones to a later time what from the nature of the work should be done first, or if he altogether omits some essential part, he is certainly not working seriously, but only pretending.

"This rule holds unalterably true whether the work be physical or not. As one cannot seriously wish to bake bread unless one first kneads the flour and then heats the brick-oven, sweeps out the ashes, and so on, so also one cannot seriously wish to lead a good life without adopting a certain order of succession in the attainment of the necessary qualities."

– Leo Tolstoy, *The First Step*

Justice seeking can follow a predictable pattern. For the sake of simplicity and clarity, I will share the entire progression of justice at the beginning of this chapter and at the end:

Attention Grabber -> Cost Weighing -> Practice -> System -> Growth -> Change -> Lasting Improvement

Attention Grabber

First we are awoken or unsettled by an "Aha!" moment or righteous anger. There has to be a catalyst that produces the desire for change – otherwise change is arbitrary and we are increasingly creating a world that is reactionary rather than revolutionary. This moment is called the "Attention Grabber" in the progression of justice.

While the Attention Grabber is often emotional and entirely effective in this regard, in order for it to last, the emotions must be gripped by some series of logical thoughts and further held accountable. The Attention Grabber must undergo a Cost Weighing stage.

Cost Weighing

This is the phase where the individual is deciding whether or not what grabbed their attention was effective and convincing enough. In the Cost Weighing stage, people are usually asking a bare minimum of two questions:

> A) "Can I do this?"

and...

B) "Is this worth it?"

There is any number of different sides of these questions that people may be exploring. The individual facets of these questions may include, but not be limited to the following:

- What will my parents/siblings/family think of me?
- Will my friends still accept me and invite me to parties and meals?
- How will I find enough food to eat?
- Is there a vegan version of XYZ food?
- Do I really have to give up all animal products?
- How do other people do this?
- Do non-human animals really feel pain?
- Are slaughterhouses that bad?

If the individual has decided all the benefits of the change outweigh the costs, the next stage is the Practice stage. This is where the Attention Grabber and any one-time actions are emotionally and mentally turned into a habit.

Practice

Habits are hard to form, yes, but older (or undesirable) habits are harder to break. This is one of the main reasons why individuals have such a challenging time embracing and remaining with veganism. Unless the new reasons and habits can outweigh the old, lasting behavior change will not manifest itself.

One of the main reasons old habits often continue to dominate is because they are not properly overridden.

In other words, in order for a smoker to quit smoking, they are most effective when they both commit to no longer smoking, and replace that action with something better every time they feel the need to smoke.

As another example, if someone is trying to lose weight and they have a bad habit of eating half a package of cookies every time they sit down in front of the TV, they will be hard-pressed and miserable if they only stop eating cookies. It becomes 20 times easier to drop that weight if they replace the cookies with carrots, whole-grain chips and hummus, fresh fruit or really anything else substantive. Then, as soon as they reach for the cookies, something else is already there, and it just so happens to be a nutritive, health-supporting choice.

The same is true of nixing non-human animal products. Instead of constantly leaning on the tried and true burger and fries next time you're out, create a visual reminder in your car or near your doorway that prompts you to make a different choice.

The Practice stage becomes strong over time and through different scenarios. For example, your new habits will become stronger through eating out with friends in addition to making different dishes at home, more so than it would through only eating new dishes at home. There is a certain reassurance and strength that comes through publically choosing vegan foods that is not present when eating solo.

System

Over more time, the Practice stage turns into the System stage. When you are no longer actively thinking about what you'll choose for lunch or dinner, what you'll say to people when they ask why you're vegan and where to go when you need food in a pinch, this is when you know you've crossed over into the System stage. In other words, the Practice becomes a System when it no longer requires conscious effort.

The Practice can only become a System if the Practice produces a desired result, or results. In other words, practicing anything will quickly become futile if the Practice itself is wrong or inadequate. The Practice must be efficient at least in the sense that it achieves or acquires what is desired – for both the practicer and any applicable recipient. Otherwise, any Practice runs the risk of falling into a no-man's-land where it has been neither disproven nor properly utilized.

This can happen as soon as 30 days in or later on. It can be contingent on meals you've had, restaurants you've been to, conversations you've had, other educational materials you've consumed and other factors, but largely it is contingent upon your own preferences and habits when working with people. Some people absorb information more readily than others; there is no right or wrong way to be human here. It is simply about the questions you have, what you feel motivated to do and then your approach for accomplishing it.

Growth

Often when the System has been in place for a few months or more, it proceeds to the Growth stage. The Growth stage is the first point at which you are able to help others see the big picture of veganism through your own story.

Growth is when you're willing to try new actions – such as leafleting, speaking, volunteering and even protesting – that you normally wouldn't have considered. The Growth stage is also where you're actively looking for opportunities to educate others on veganism.

This does not necessarily mean you're talking to everyone about veganism all the time. No, in fact, you're looking for timely and even tasteful ways to educate others. It's when you're in a mindset that seeks mental, emotional and verbal doorways that are already open, so you can accomplish more good for the vegan cause. As you can see, the Growth stage involves exactly that: growing into new places and habits that otherwise wouldn't have crossed your mind. It also involves and typically requires leaving your comfort zone.

Change

After the Growth stage comes the Change stage. The title of this stage is not always to be taken literally – because the change you made towards veganism multiple steps ago has already become rooted. What the Change stage means is you've become adjusted to the ever-shifting, ever-growing face of activism and veganism so much that you're anticipating Change and maximally facilitating it.

In other words, you're viewing the entire world through a vegan lens by default – or at least viewing the world as inevitably becoming vegan. This is where some of the best growth and change actually happens. For example, when you go out to eat with friends or family, what's on the menu is no longer simply depressing you. You're viewing all the selections and creating vegan versions in your head – thereby having an easier time showing other people how wonderful veganism is.

The Change stage is also where your family and close friends know, understand and accept that you are vegan without further thought. Another way of thinking about it is that upon reaching the Change stage, veganism is now associated with your identity on the root level. People no longer have to guess that you're vegan or wonder what it is about; they've seen you in action long enough, in word and deed, and any ambiguity has been wiped away through persistent action and public identification as a vegan.

Lasting Improvement

Finally, Lasting Improvement is the stage where all previous mentalities, actions and habits have been erased and replaced by new ones. It is the stage where every conscious thought you have leads to a conscious manifestation of justice. You're openly, willingly and freely rejecting injustice and actively pursuing and rooting as many forms of justice as possible.

Christ calls us to not let our thinking be patterned after the world in Romans 12:2. In order to consummate and manifest the fullest, deepest version of justice, we must look beyond the cheap, shallow definitions of justice the world attempts to perpetuate.

In order to bring fellow Christians and non-Christians along with us into the new realm of justice, we must not remove freedom of choice, but rather *illuminate the utter power of the choice we are given.* In other words, authentic freedom and justice are not made manifest through eliminating all but once choice, but through meticulously illustrating how one choice is infinitely better than all others.

After all, we must be defined by love, as is detailed in 1 John 4:13-16. What's more, the truest definition of our love will come from God the Father – a sacrificial, all-consuming love that has no shortcomings. To love fully and to love deeply, we must look to our Father as the ultimate example of how to continue against all odds and opposition.

Here is the entire justice system progression again:

Attention Grabber -> Cost Weighing -> Practice -> System -> Growth -> Change -> Lasting Improvement

Chapter 6 Thesis:

Seeking justice – and living it out – has to be condensed down to a practical, simple enough system, otherwise we run the risk of falling back into patterns of injustice, whether we want to or not. Creating a lifestyle that prioritizes justice is not impossible or too difficult; one simply needs the right tools and mindsets to facilitate action across an extended period of time so it can become habitual and second nature.

"All growth depends upon activity. There is no development physically or intellectually without effort, and effort means work." – Calvin Coolidge

Chapter 7: The Christian Requisite To Serve And Appreciate Others

"A good character is the best tombstone. Those who loved you and were helped by you will remember you when forget-me-nots have withered. Carve your name on hearts, not on marble." – Charles Spurgeon

Our global culture is losing the servant mentality rapidly. In fact, most days it's hard to believe we ever had it at all. Materialism and consumerism have seemingly devoured every corner of the world, leaving the small pockets of those pitted against such evils in difficult times.

There's no mistaking it: true service of others and consumerism are forever at odds. The desire to do more for others with less and the desire to constantly acquire more for oneself are like black and white; mutually exclusive. As soon as you progress towards more of one, you're necessitating less of the other.

To follow Christ requires the appreciation and service of others. Christ Himself acknowledged that this would not be easy or even readily desirable at all times. Heck, there are dozens of passages in the New Testament alone about how Jews and Gentiles are encouraged to get along.

Since the dawn of humanity, we've often tried to become friends with one another while battling the internal fear that "others" only represent some kind of threat. We've selected the silliest reasons to separate ourselves from other people – religious belief, skin color, gender, perceived ability and more – and this mindset is what has caused countless ills throughout recorded history.

Jews and Gentiles, just like all other groups of people, are supposed to get along. It's how a greater world is built. And yet, people (myself included) lose vision and make up excuses, and we find ourselves back at square one. The question of this chapter stands: **How can we as Christians serve others, as well as**

our own, better?

I see a few pillars of behavior through which we can once again restore and magnify the importance of serving others:

How can we serve others better?

- Creating and seeking out more opportunities to interact with those we don't know as well
- In relation to the above, minimizing or eliminating assumptions
- Learning to be content with less – The quest for more "stuff" directly impedes growing relational depth
- "You become more like that which you gaze upon" – To ditch our desire for "more," we must look to the King of All

How Christians Can Truly Embody The Servant Heart

The ultimate and most important definition of a servant is one who puts others before him or herself. A servant is someone that sees a need, even if unspoken, and moves swiftly and compassionately to fill that need. There are countless reasons why Jesus was the ideal servant, but we will break down just a few.

The Woman At The Well

Jesus was on His way back to Galilee and had to pass through Samaria. Israel had been divided into two kingdoms years ago, which is what led to the division and hatred between Samaritans and Jews, but this is all we need to understand for the present story to make sense.

While on His way back, He stopped at a well for a break, and a Samaritan woman happened to be there as well. By Jesus' ensuing request for a drink from her bucket, He was breaking down walls that other people wouldn't dare interfere with.

Jesus was far more interested in the person than upholding any sort of invalid cultural taboo or that they were physically proximal to each other. Even though Jesus was the one asking for a drink of water, He was actually serving her twofold.

For starters, the fact that He struck up a conversation with her established a powerful cultural message. He was showing that He wasn't afraid of her reputation or His in having a normal conversation. It just so happens that this woman had led a life of infidelity, so most Jews would have been doubly sure to avoid her. Jesus didn't care about any of this because He was on a completely different mission: show love to her and give her the Good News.

Later on in their discussion, Jesus mentioned He was the Messiah:

25 "The woman said, ... I do know that the Messiah is coming. When he arrives, we'll get the whole story." 26 "I am he," said Jesus. "You don't have to wait any longer or look any further." (John 4:25-26)

By having conversations with people like this – watching over the unseen and unloved – we can healthfully and appropriately imitate Jesus and continually build a world of trust, unity and mutual success.

The Raw Need For Service

We need to get our hands dirty! Metaphorically and literally. The truest Christian life was never designed for sterile comfort, just tossing a few dollars at a collection plate every week and counting that as having "done your part." No; deep, genuine Christian life is about much more than that.

It's not to say that every Christian needs to drop what they're doing and all of a sudden become missionaries in under-developed countries. But a real commitment to Christ is reflected in every area of a Christian's life. Every area means *every area*.

It's not enough to attend church on the weekends, bring your kids to Bible summer camp and call it a day. The committed Christian must be devoted in thought, habit, word and deed. This requires a lot of diligence on the part of the Christian, which is how we grow closer to God in the first place.

Sometimes it's almost as though Christians have a "for credit" view on service; as though if you work hard on a specific project or with a group long enough, that you've earned the right to kick back and watch others do the work for a bit. Christian service, and a servant's heart in general, was never meant to be like this. One's heart, especially as a Christian, must be so eager and thrilled to serve that the very act becomes attractive in its own sake – not because of any tangible reward or supposed merit.

Are We Building Freedom And Unity, Or Entitlement And Enslavement?

We also need to watch our environment(s) and what cues we take from them. In other words, the people surrounding us as we volunteer and our reasons for volunteering/serving are just as important as the work itself.

We can ask our teams and ourselves the following questions as we approach new serving opportunities or enhance existing ones:

- From who or what?
- How/when/why are we implementing these?
- How effective are they?
- Are they the right/wrong ones?
- What are the results/effects?

How The Rich Become Desensitized To The Poor

The more material possessions you have in life, the more you want and the more entitled/less grateful you feel. The less you have, the less you need and the more grateful you become.

Think about how long non-human animals have been serving humans without complaint. Ultimately this has been for as long as it's happened in recorded history, and this may be longer than humans admit or acknowledge. But the overall point is that non-human animals, being completely defenseless against any cruel human intent, have no choice but to comply with evil desires.

The same thing happens in regards to the rich and the poor – or, better put, the materially wealthy and the materially destitute. Not all who obtain opulence are truly rich, and not all who are given humble physical blessings are poor, but that is a different story for a different time. The point is that the rich take advantage of the poor in the same way we humans take advantage of non-human animals. We force them to do our bidding simply because we are in a position of power – neglecting the virtue-laden responsibilities that come with our dominion and opting for comfort and greed instead. This self-satisfaction and overkill will be our permanent undoing if we do not holistically correct our course.

What's The Story You've Been Told?

During our childhood years, we are told by our parents and general caretakers that some non-human animals should be celebrated and even paraded, and other non-human animals deserve only to be on our dinner plate. We're told some non-human animals – cats, dogs, hamsters, gerbils and the like – are appropriate choices for pets, and other non-human animals – cows, pigs, chickens and sheep – are there for us to exploit for personal gain.

Oftentimes, we end up believing these misconceptions and not challenging them until someone prompts us to do so later. As I've shared elsewhere in this book, this first component of the story is not our fault – unless we ignore the responsibility that comes with being given new knowledge.

Living in clarity of action requires examining our values. It's worth taking a few minutes right now to contemplate your own answers to the following questions:

- What *are* **my** values?

  _____

  _____

  _____

  _____

- Have I adopted the values that my family and friends already hold?

  _____

  _____

  _____

  _____

- Is this a good or bad thing? Is it a neutral thing? Why?

  _____

  _____

  _____

- How do I want to see my values in action?

_____

_____

_____

_____

- Do my actions already represent my values? If not, what might I do to change this?

_____

_____

_____

_____

- Am I content when my values are only used on occasion? Am I most content when my values are used on a consistent, even daily basis?

_____

_____

_____

- Do I desire to add any other values to my existing set of values? What might they be and how can I implement them? Who or what inspired me to do this?

_____

_____

_____

_____

"Believe your beliefs and doubt your doubts... If not, you will doubt your beliefs and believe your doubts." – Tony Robbins

Picture Your Own Cat Or Dog In Slaughterhouse Conditions

It's an absolutely ghastly mental image, but it certainly gets the point across. It's complete injustice and it must be stopped at all costs.

Vegan activist Gary Yourofsky often states, "Regular slaughterhouses today contain animals, and nobody bats an eye. Yet if you replaced those animals with humans, you've just reinvented Birkenau or Auschwitz."

When mass atrocities are committed, people barely pay attention. When an individual or single non-human animal receives any kind of news coverage, people go berserk.

When given a picture of a piglet or a calf, most people comment on how cute and adorable he or she looks, and may mention picturing the non-human animal on a bright, sunny, green farm, with the most joyful, carefree life imaginable.

Tragically, this imagination could not be further from the truth. 97 to 99 percent of all commercially available non-human animal products come from Concentrated Animal Feeding Operation farms, or CAFOs for short.* CAFOs are where most non-human animals spend their agonized, tormented lives before being brought to the slaughterhouse, where corporate mistakes are routinely overlooked and the creatures are killed in a bloody, grotesque mass of panic.

Chapter 7 Thesis:

As Christians we must take the action systems and mindsets we've learned throughout this book and apply it to other areas of the world. Compassion, love, goodness, patience, hope and justice can be brought to all corners of the world needing these virtues, and veganism is the ideal bedrock through which to prop up consistently effective systems of justice and real growth. Christians are called to lead the charge for justice through veganism, lest other, lesser definitions of justice settle for weak, impotent results.

"To a man whose mind is free there is something even more intolerable in the sufferings of animals than in the sufferings of man. For with the latter it is at least admitted that suffering is evil and that the man who causes it is a criminal. But thousands of animals are uselessly butchered every day without a shadow of remorse. If any man were to refer to it, he would be thought ridiculous. And that is the unpardonable crime." – Romain Rolland

Chapter 8: Being A Good Steward, Especially Of The Earth

"There's enough in the world for everyone's need, but not for everyone's greed." – Dale Partridge, keynote speaker, entrepreneur, consultant and author of *People Over Profit*

When I first saw the deepest, truest side of how horribly we are treating our world, I was surprised too. Actually, "surprised" barely does the situation justice. I was appalled, aghast and in complete disbelief.

Most people I know – in fact, every individual I can consciously call to mind – cares about the wellbeing of the Earth. I've never met anyone personally who has a direct interest in causing greater ills to befall our beautiful, green world. The dilemma therefore quickly rises when we witness a further, larger side of the truth that causes direct tension with our current daily choices.

Before I go into the deep end of this chapter, I want to share a nugget that brought me great clarity *and* encouragement a number of years ago. I was consuming some form of media when I came across the following statement:

"No single individual will kill the Earth because they didn't recycle a plastic water bottle, and no single individual will save the Earth because they picked it up off the street."

The point of this thought is to illuminate the fact that helping (and hurting) the Earth (and all within it) is not done by a single entity. No, both the detriments *and* progress seen within our world are caused by waves of action comprised of individuals, on the simplest level.

Every single day, we are either helping the Earth (and ourselves) flourish, or we are causing destruction. We're either looking out for everyone, or we're only looking out for ourselves. The scientific community holds consensus around the fact that matter cannot be removed – only altered – but that does not mean our Earth is impervious to our actions. In fact, it's the exact opposite. All actions we take today as humans have direct or indirect results tomorrow.

When considering veganism, many folks have concern over the following:

A) Whether there's enough food to feed the world
B) How to make sure non-human animal farmers don't lose their jobs because of veganism
C) How to preserve state and national parks and other reserves/wetlands
D) What all the animals would do if/when we stopped eating them

While it's not within the scope of this book to handle all these questions in detail, I will briefly cover them for the sake of making a holistic, sound argument for each. For further reading on these concerns, I recommend *Meat Logic* by Charles Horn.

A) Is There Enough Food To Feed The World?

Yes. We are currently producing enough food worldwide to feed about 10 billion people.* Tragically, we only need to produce food for 7.5 billion people, and to make matters worse, 1 billion or more people go hungry every day, due to a variety of factors.*

These factors can include governmental corruption, lack of resources, lack of access to education, lack of clean water and more* – all of which can fall under the umbrella of abject poverty.* We are producing more than enough food for everyone; we simply live in a world where currently, not everyone who needs food is able to obtain it.

B) Won't Farmers Lose Their Entire Livelihood?

Kinda yes, mostly no. The situation here can be grouped into two components. First, if and when the meat, dairy and egg industries completely fall out of business, farmers aren't going to wake up one Monday morning and all of a sudden notice that their business is no longer viable.

They'll have seen it coming: From news reports, headlines, TV shows, movies, documentaries, their weekly or monthly financial documents, stockholders, stakeholders, their managers or business owners, their friends, family and their own trips to the grocery store. Despite having unlimited access to information while still living in a world where people (often) don't pay attention to the most important things, we don't live in *so much* of a vacuum that we don't see things coming.

What have people in other industries done when their businesses or careers collapsed? They went and found new jobs, or started new enterprises. It really is that simple.

Secondly, farmers who used to exploit non-human animals for their flesh, secretions and babies could easily switch their resources to farm vegetables, grains and fruits. It's already been shown that veganic farming is 15-16 times more resource effective than non-human animal farming,* meaning the yields of vegan farmers outshine even the most efficient non-human animal farmer.

C) I Care A Lot About Upholding Nature Preserves. What Can We Do About Them?

As mentioned previously, essentially everyone I know cares about the Earth, and that includes nature preserves. We want to see our Earth preserved for decades, even centuries to come, so our children and grandchildren can have the same (or better) experiences.

Sadly, once again, the choices most of us make three times a day (or more) at the table are in direct conflict with the care for the Earth we profess. As I've shared elsewhere in the book, when people are truly unaware of the facts, it's not immediately their fault.

However, as soon as an individual becomes aware of what's happening and how it's happening, they are linked to responsibility for that problem. In the same way that an onlooker towards a house pet or young child being abused must stand up to injustice, the individual who is aware of the atrocities of factory farming and the entire non-human animal exploitation industry must stand up against violence and bloodshed.

According to the International Livestock Research Institute, livestock already covers 45 percent of the Earth's total land.* For easy (and realistic) math, that's half the land on Earth. *Half.*

Quite insane, when you think about it. But any reason for which livestock would be using so much land must be legitimate. And yet, as we peel back the layers of the onion, we find this is not the case.

After examining the former fact alone, eradicating animal agriculture would automatically produce more land gains than any other single action. If the world went vegan overnight, that would produce more land restoration than any other single action that all individuals could take today. There's no other sweeping action a government or business could take that would restore land for other purposes than reducing and/or eliminating animal agriculture.

To put it another way, the priority should not be about finding land to pay to preserve; it should be about leading a lifestyle that produces as little waste and damage as possible in the first place. Veganism is this lifestyle.

For those who are earnestly concerned about preserving land, the most logical thing to do is remove any consumer demand (via your dollars when purchasing anything, especially food) you have that acts against genuine land preservation.

D) What Would All The Non-Human Animals Do If We Stopped Eating Them?

The answer here is the same as the answer with farmers. Non-human animals aren't going to take over the Earth if and when we stop eating them. We'll simply be producing less of them in the first place.

The only reason millions of non-human animals are already killed for food every week is because worldwide demand necessitates these deaths. In other words, as demand goes down, so does supply. Price would go up, but this component of the equation is irrelevant, since all we're talking about is whether or not we'd have a non-human animal surplus on our hands. The answer is we wouldn't.

Taking Personal Responsibility

It's easy to look at the world, see the state we're in and throw one's hands up in disgust or deep sadness. The world is incredibly broken – with problems stacked 10 miles high – and it's completely understandable that it appears beyond repair. The truth is, some issues might be beyond repair, but the majority of struggles we still face are mendable.

As I've mentioned previously in the book, it's not the juggernauts and giant corporate forces of the world that cause most changes and structural shifts – it's the collective of individuals. The world won't career over the edge of collapse by producing one more plastic water bottle, but it won't be saved by recycling one more.

Many of us, myself included, often look at a problem and think it's too big for any individual to make a significant difference. This is a lie fed to us by our own minds as well as the media at large. Hundreds of media outlets often only instill fear and discouragement in the hearts of millions by only talking about how things are getting worse. There's little to zero talk about how and why individuals can take a stand against destruction of the Earth and corporate greed.

All of it begins with taking personal responsibility.

That's why you, reader, are not off the hook. No one is off the hook.

In order to initiate and establish lasting change, every single individual must take into account his or her personal habits. It's here where we apply the Maya Angelou logic of "If you know better, you should do better."

Publications from the *American Dietetic Association,* the *Stanford Environmental Law Review* and *Environmental Protection Agency* don't lie. If trusted experts openly share the fact that a vegan diet is suitable for all stages of life and that animal agriculture is the single largest cause of all environmental ills, we're foolish to ignore such life-altering proclamations.

Why To Start Now

Life happens here and now. Yes, we have the past to learn from and the future to look forward to, but the only moment that can be fully seized is the present.

People often get stuck up on matters of justice because they fall for two lies:

A) I'm only one person, so my impact can't possibly mean that much
B) There's not enough time to fix all the wrongs in the world, so we might as well not even try

Both of these lies are understandable, but can be thwarted and conquered. First off, the "I'm just one person" idea is entirely a myth. Scientists have found that even the most introverted person can influence up to 10,000 people across their lifetime – and that's a conservative estimate.

What's more, one person can do a lot – a lot more than most people realize, anyway. Vegans can save 100-200 land animals a year just through their eating habits.* That's a lot of good being done just by taking meat, cheese, milk and eggs off the plate.

Chapter 8 Thesis:

Veganism is the simplest and most effective answer to the problems currently degrading our Earth. Christians can rely on the foundational habits of veganism to uphold and preserve the sanctity of nature that still remains, as well as counteract any ills that various profit-driven interests and other evils perpetuate through their ruthless indifference of Earth's inherent beauty and abundance. However, Christians must not become complacent; we must adopt veganism for ourselves first and then encourage it in others, especially those who are receptive to a message of holistic justice.

"I submit that an individual who breaks a law that conscience tells him is unjust and who willingly accepts the penalty of imprisonment in order to rouse the conscience of the community over its injustice is in reality expressing the highest respect for the law." – Dr. Martin Luther King, Jr.

Chapter 9: Seeking Truth Consummately As A Christian

"Truth is so obscure in these times, and falsehood so established, that, unless we love the truth, we cannot know it." – Blaise Pascal

The Importance Of Being "In The Know"

Everyone loves to be "in the know." It's how you can feel important, accepted, appreciated, even admired. We want to know what's going on, especially with our friends and family. To our credit, it's important to do this with those we love – both for them and ourselves.

Perhaps some people may think being in the know is somewhat of a pretentious thing, but this is not the case, nor should it be, at least when taken within the right context. There are some things within life none of us can ever know, and there are some things many of us need not ever know. But there are plenty of things that most of us should know (or strive to know), and that's what this section is about.

To be the fullest Christians we can be, it's vital to be consummate truth seekers. We must always be pushing the boundaries of what can be known, so that we can grow closer to God in this process.

Thousands of people who lived in prior times simply accepted authority's word on much of the freedom and decision-making in their lives. Truth be told, this reality is still present today. Most people do not challenge someone in an authority position, simply because they are within an authority position (see Stanley Milgram). There's something about perceived power that can almost always control a group of people.

There are countless more studies one can research on the topic of power, control, subjugation and influence, but this is not the book to explore such a topic at length. The present point is that most of us, Christian or not, simply accept authority's word because it appears more powerful and necessary than our own.

Why is this? Well, there are at least a few basic reasons. First, the simplest reason is that humans seek to avoid pain. This is true of everyone, regardless of whether or not you consider yourself against the grain (in any fashion). Standing up and speaking out against authority figures, even if for justifiable reasons, requires stepping out of your comfort zone. Even when you're pushing to move justice forward in the world, challenging those in other positions of power and attempting to present contrary information is a bold move.

A second and related reason is because speaking out against an authority figure (or injustice) almost invariably means you'll soon discover which friends truly side with you (and which do not). This can be an even more painful reality for some, because one's strongest social circle is an immediate and highly individualized source of strength, acceptance, validation and support.

These two reasons alone are often more than enough to keep many Christians at bay. This can sound like a harsh statement, but I say it out of love, not out of condemnation. Aspects of full love require tough love, and countless are the times when self-professed Christians have taken a step back instead of taking a step forward.

Before I go any further, it's essential to reiterate that I am nowhere near a perfect man. I have stood back more times than I can count, as well. However, what I've realized is that my actions as a human are simply a reflection of the faith I have in my Creator. What does it say about us as Christians if our default move is one of retreat rather than engagement?

I cannot imagine it represents anything with sincere congruence. If we truly are the Christians we claim to be, our actions must be marked by risk for a cause, rather than that of self-preservation.

Biblical writer Paul said the body will fade away, but the spirit lives on in Romans 8:10. The Bible also says the world may attempt to take our lives, but who can actually take our soul? No one. At least, no one but God has the right or the authority to interact with anyone's soul. So, this should be a clear and powerful reminder that we have nothing to fear when the world attempts to shut us down or hide the truth, because the true source of life (our souls) cannot be messed with.

So what does consummate truth-seeking mean?

- Being committed to the truth, because the ultimate Truth is that from which our very life extends
- Having a genuine love for the truth to such an extent that we *desire* to seek it
- Implementing the truth we discover into our lives; living by truth on principle, not merely rhetoric or face value appeasement
- Being willing to continually test the truth to see how true it is
- Understanding that extremely few people understand, appreciate and seek out the truth, and that conflict (or tension) will naturally arise from this

- Including love with truth whenever possible (in action and communication) such that truth is not brutally loveless, and that love is not hypocritical

Regularly Challenging Oneself

Now that we've set the stage for the basics of being a consummate truth seeker, we must apply a practical framework to the discovery, testing and implementation of truth.

To do this section justice, one must embrace the concept that university professor Steven Sample has popularized. It's true that some things in life reside within a black-or-white scale. In other words, some aspects of reality are either this or that, up or down, right or wrong. An example of this would be your current body position. You are either standing somewhere or you are not. You may be laying down, sitting in a chair or crouched over, but any of these options would mean by default you are not standing.

Most aspects of life, however, are gray. They simply cannot be condensed down to a binary. Eating avocados, while healthy for just about every person I can imagine, may not be a taste or texture everyone likes. And this is totally fine. Some people are allergic to avocados too. Finding employment at a veterinary clinic, while extremely fulfilling for a few individuals, would never suit other individuals. Wearing minimalistic, non-brand-name clothing, while reviled by some, may be heartily embraced by others. Most people don't think about these kinds of things unless prompted with the thought. Yet, when presented with the premise, most people would agree that yes, what suits others does not necessarily suit them.

The difficult bit about all this is that countless folks (myself included, at times) prefer a life where everything can be assigned to a binary. This makes life easier but it frankly rarely makes life better, or even right. Also, the end significance of virtually all decisions within life should be weighed by the context in which you want to make the decision.

"You're wrong; I'm right. That person doesn't know what they're talking about; I do. This is the right decision for me, but not for you."

Such are the possible statements that float through various minds, depending on the individual and the context. Assigning virtually all moments of pain in life to a binary is itself an attempt to escape as much pain as possible. In other words, putting everything on a "right-or-wrong, on-or-off" switch in life makes it less painful to make decisions – whether the result of those decisions is actually correct or not.

Checking Stories And Statements Against The Bible

In order to both know the most important book in the Christian faith and defend attacks against it, we as Christians must know our Bibles. The Bible is the first and final authority on how Christians should learn from God, help others see His truth and construct (or deconstruct) lifestyle choices. Hebrews 4:12 says: "God means what He says. What He says goes. His powerful Word is sharp as a surgeon's scalpel, cutting through everything, whether doubt or defense, laying us open to listen and obey. Nothing and no one is

184

impervious to God's Word. We can't get away from it—no matter what."

These are relatively confrontational words. **If an individual lives their life far away from the truth, the truth itself will seem like hell.** In order to grow deeper with God's word, as well as know how we can continually live it out more effectively, we must assess our current standing with the Word.

A great question to ask yourself is, **"What is my existing core knowledge about the Bible?"** This is naturally a broad question, but can bring you up to speed on areas you know less about. Simply reading one chapter per day, every day, has been a major life habit of mine over the past few years. It's simple enough such that you can accomplish it with low resistance, but it's essential and effective enough such that you grow a bit every day and come closer to God.

A second fantastic question to ask is, **"Who are my most frequent human sources of Biblical teaching?"** In other words, which humans (or groups of humans) do you most frequently turn to for more information on God's word? This could be a church, a podcast, a blog, all three or even something/someone else.

It's important for us to evaluate the human sources through which we learn more about our Almighty and Perfect Creator. Humans are flawed, but God is not. Therefore, through the salvation and sanctification provided via Jesus Christ, Christians are always becoming a bit more like God while on Earth, but none of us can achieve perfection while still human.

The best Christian leaders are those who are humble enough to keep learning and courageous enough to keep sharing. If you notice any Christian leaders who are exemplifying the following traits (especially those you interact with often), you should **definitely** be cautious:

- Favoritism or cronyism
- Seeking or supporting the idea of minimal accountability
- Irrational outbursts of anger, sexual advances or other grave misconduct
- Blatantly bloated pride or arrogance
- Secretive communication or lack of/poor communication skills altogether
- Expecting others to lead by example without doing it themselves
- Constantly trying to get their way without listening to others
- Marginalizing people and avoiding the time, attention and care it takes to develop individuals

Now, I know not everyone is in a position to speak to a leader about concerns they have, but at the very least, you can share your thoughts with someone else you do trust, and consider how you might be able to find someone else to follow.

In any case, the choice to follow a different leader should be a conscious one. It doesn't necessarily need to be a slow transition, but it should be a thoughtful one.

The Bible Is God's Inerrant Word

Many Christians desire to hear, understand and apply God's word correctly. Nobody wants to "get it wrong" on purpose. Yet, as Christians, we often struggle with applying Biblical truth as diligently as we should.

Much of this comes down to trusting the Bible, and a quick history lesson can explain everything even better. As art has progressed throughout recorded history, humans have constantly been sharing it and attempting to interpret it (especially across cultural boundaries). In the 1960s, a gentleman named Jacques Derrida came along and introduced the idea of deconstructionism. The concept represents the idea that individual observers can view a piece of art or text and decide for themselves what it means.

In other words, deconstructionism stands in direct opposition to empirical truth. Deconstructionism can look at a paragraph and say, "Here's what it means to me," where someone committed to learning and applying the truth would say, "Here's what the paragraph is actually saying; now, how does that apply to reality within my life?"

To elucidate further, we can examine the shocking reality present in many churches across the United States. It's all too common to hear in small groups after reading a Bible passage, "What is this verse saying to you?" While this question is not far off from the truth, it contains a critical deviation that should not be overlooked.

Instead of a small group leader asking what the passage means to those in the group, everyone should be reading the Bible for the inherent truth it contains. Then, when the truth is derived from the passage, the truth should be applied to the life of the individual. For example, 2 Timothy 1:7 says the following:

"God doesn't want us to be shy with His gifts, but bold and loving and sensible."

The question should not be, "What is this saying to me?" It should be, "How can I take the truth about being bold, loving and sensible, and make my life a better reflection of these characteristics?"

So, in direct relevance with applying Biblical truth to our lives, we have to trust the ultimate source, otherwise we are essentially only kidding ourselves. You either believe the Bible is exactly how God intended it, or you do not. You either trust and follow God as your absolute best guide, or you do not. You cannot half-trust God.

Open-Handed And Closed-Hand Issues

Christians cannot really get anywhere in the world (especially with one another) if we have only open- or closed-hand issues. We need both types of issues to stand for our convictions, and to make progress on the things we care about.

Open-handed issues can be described as topics upon which a few educated opinions have been formed within an individual's heart and mind, but where more information and discussion can (and should) be had. Hopefully veganism lands here for most Christians, if it is not already a personal conviction.

Closed-handed issues can be described as topics upon which little to no discussion can be had – at least, no discussion will change an individual's convictions about a matter.

Within Christian circles, we have to more effectively and appropriately have these discussions and create room for the results of these discussions to be carried out. The world will not pay any further attention to Christians (they already ignore us pretty well) if all we do is continue fighting over needless frustrations, rather than teaming up where we can and working with each other on the rest.

Implicit Egotism And Cultural Standards

Implicit egotism, which everyone has, is the concept that you naturally seek out ideas, places, people and things that remind you of yourself. In other words, a human's natural bent is to further reinforce the idea of oneself by looking for experiences, objects and other humans that innately remind them of themselves.

As mentioned above, everyone deals with implicit egotism because it's simply human nature. We often see no reason to go out of our way to change our natural patterns of ourselves, because we often see no reason to change *ourselves*. We often don't want to change ourselves because we see or experience little that actually effects legitimate change over a long enough period of time.

Implicit egotism isn't necessarily a root of destruction. However, it can be deadly if it impedes moral progress in an individual's life or the life of society. Implicit egotism has the capacity to be deadly because it can keep someone in his or her comfort zone too long.

We Christians have to watch implicit egotism carefully because it can support two things:

1. Sin, and
2. Lack of unity, whether with ourselves or the world

Be open to the idea that humans – even Christians – can get things wrong more often than we might think. In fact, I'd say Christians get it wrong more often than most other humans. This is one of the main reasons many non-Christians have a mistrust and dislike of Christians (see *unChristian* by David Kinnaman).

Implicit egotism can stand in the way of true progress because it can keep otherwise great and unique people from one another. When fantastic individuals are kept apart, it can wreck what potential innovation may have sprung up, solely because we humans judge aesthetically so often.

We need to know what we truly stand for, what we truly value, in order to know what we're going to hold fast to, and what we're willing to change.

Ask yourself these questions, answer honestly (of course) and take notes (especially if you feel highly motivated to do so):

- What do I stand for?

_____

_____

_____

- No, what do I **actually** stand for, as an individual?

_____

_____

_____

_____

- What does it mean to "stand for" something? What does it mean to "sit for" something?

_____

_____

_____

_____

- What have I been told to stand for by my family?

_____

_____

_____

_____

- What have I been told to stand for by my friends?

_____

_____

_____

_____

- What have I been told to stand for by my teachers, supervisors, leaders and other key influencers in my direct personal life (no influencers you don't personally know or interact with, i.e. Internet peeps)?

_____

_____

_____

_____

- What do I *want* to stand for?

_____

_____

_____

_____

- How well have I been doing with this?

_____

_____

_____

_____

- Is there something I need to let go of?

_____

_____

_____

_____

- Who can I talk with to learn more about this conviction?

_____

_____

_____

_____

- What am I going to have to give up in order to progress with this goal?

_____

_____

_____

_____

Look At The Leader(s) Of A Church

It's beyond dispute that the primary leader and leadership structure of a church reveals the primary demographic of the church as well. You attract more of who you already are, and churches are no exception.

What does this mean in light of a Christian vegan book? For starters, embracing a vegan life already means you're aiming to embrace all people, creatures and cultures at all times. It doesn't always mean you'll

194

understand everything perfectly (in fact, you'll be learning every step of the way, as I am), but your life will become incredibly rich far sooner and deeper than you ever thought possible.

Keep in mind that great leaders openly seek out ways to be demographically and culturally diverse. The best leaders of the past, present and future make every step oriented around acknowledging all groups of people. Particularly in a Christian worldview, we cannot afford to leave anyone in the dust. Not only can we not afford it, we are scorned if we do. Christ's love embraces and redeems people of all backgrounds, so we must extend the same grace.

Leadership, like many other critical embarkations, is a delicate balance. While seeking to pour your trust and openness into leaders of integrity, take leaders with a grain of salt. We should naturally strive to trust our leaders and comrades as deeply as possible, but as Christian humans, our first, fullest and greatest trust should be in God.

While we all remain on Earth, we are naturally going to have to work with and trust each other as much as possible. We can reach very deep levels of this, and I see it happening all the time, which is beautiful and incredibly encouraging. Let us stride forward in the confidence given to us by Christ, and lift each other up in truth, integrity and love given to us by the Father.

Don't Defend A Tradition Just Because It's A Tradition

Perhaps the worst thing a Christian can do is simply defend a tradition for its own sake. This is akin to pretending a coworker's illegal behavior is acceptable just because they've been doing it for months, or years.

A wrong is a wrong is a wrong. It takes gumption and raw courage to appropriately attack improper behavior or circumstances, but the committed Christian understands it must be done.

Defending a tradition for familiarity alone is often the root of evil (or at least unhelpful) actions. Slave owners defended their "perceived right" to keep treating their slaves a certain way. Men defended their "perceived right" to keep women under their thumb economically and socially. Specific religious and social groups have defended their "perceived right" to oppress gays, lesbians, transgenders and bisexuals on the basis of their sexual orientation and nothing more.

All of these oppressive groups have acted out of one box: hateful ignorance. More specifically, all of the groups that felt wrongfully threatened were trying to defend some kind of tradition, which was simply their own personal comfort – nothing more.

Once again, this is not to make it sound like all Christians have gotten it wrong, or that there aren't good things happening in the world in general. Of course there are great things happening, and with patience and persistence, Christians can continue working with those of other faiths and beliefs to build a world we all want.

When a tradition is in question, we must examine the tradition – ruthlessly, even – to see if it is justified at all. There never existed a period of the world where "tradition for tradition alone" was ever justified, but it's certainly not permissible now.

If the tradition in question is justified, strengthen it. Add the angle of your personal conviction to the framework through which you first discovered it. Strengthening an existing tradition through your own conviction allows you to build action into a legacy that can help even more people in the future.

If the tradition is unjustified, begin stripping it away and replacing it with something else. Anything that's unjust needs to go. Otherwise, you risk the injustice being associated with your character. In the instance of Thanksgiving (highly personal for me as well), the scenario that's all too common is that people don't question the food that's on the table. Time is being spent with family, positive emotions have already filled the room and people generally don't want to disrupt what has been a source of comfort and familiarity for years (possibly decades).

Quick Conversation Recommendations

Now, I'm not saying you should all of a sudden break the silence (or the merriment) and simply start talking about factory farming or unnecessary violence in general with nothing to lead on. People rarely take to new information well if the situation has not been personalized, with some buy-in from everyone at the table.

There's reason to be polite and considerate of peoples' desire to eat food and be full for the night. Even though your closest family members and loved ones may well be consuming the body parts of dead creatures, you don't need to shatter every semblance of decency within the room by creating discontent (or even tears) out of context.

People are best approached with difficult and even conflicting information when the appropriate context has been established. This can be done one-on-one or even in group settings away from the dinner table. Angry as you may be for seeing a non-human animal used unjustly for "food" (and valid as you are in such a stance), there is a time and place for indignation, and it's often best away from the dinner table.

It's possible to be an effective vegan (or advocate for any cause) while still maintaining sincere friendships and familial relationships. If family members or friends approach you first with genuine questions in mind, give them your honest, graceful and truthful answers. This is the ideal scenario, as you haven't had to do any "selling" of the vegan message. People have taken notice of what you deem worthy, and their curiosity has been sparked.

If people don't come to you first, still feel free to approach them about your thoughts. It's often best to bring your questions to someone who you think will be willing to listen and dialogue as honestly as you will. You don't want to go to someone who will most likely just treat the conversation with contempt or utter disinterest.

Back To Traditions...

Here is my personal framework for examining a tradition for validity:

- What intrinsic value does the tradition seek to maintain on a ground level?
- Who have I "learned" or "absorbed" the tradition from? Family, friends, coworkers?
- What does the tradition seek to perpetuate? Actions, behaviors, tastes, comforts?
- Is the tradition already aligned with my existing values as an individual? (This requires more self-reflection)
- Am I genuinely excited about the tradition as is? Can I see myself recommending it or passing it along to friends or my (potential) family?
- What do people gain by this tradition remaining in place?
- What do people lose if this tradition is removed?
- What do other creatures/entities lose or gain if this tradition is removed/remains?
- Does this tradition exploit anyone or anything vulnerable? If so, why, and are there alternatives to the current state of the tradition?
- Am I threatened or mocked for challenging the tradition? If so, why?

The Gospel Is Truly Uncomfortable

At the end of the day, the Gospel really is uncomfortable. If it's not uncomfortable to you – Christian or not – you don't have an accurate picture of it yet.

It's the reality that God, the creator of the Universe, provided a perfect way for us sinful humans to be with Him forever, at the cost of a life not ours. In order to be a Christian, one must consciously and willingly give up any right to our own fleshly motives and desires, in order to follow Christ at all costs.

In the words of Andy Mineo, "Christianity isn't complex, it's just costly." To put it another way, the actual "mechanics" of Christianity are pretty straightforward, but the level of involvement required to truly follow Christ is 100 percent and nothing less.

This is certainly one reason people reject or avoid Christianity. Christ, in return for giving you a forgiven soul and eternity in Heaven, asks of you your life. There is no way to beat around the bush here, and in the end you fall on one side of the fence or another.

While the Gospel is in its own category of importance, many other areas of life hold the same solemnity and stark contrast. Either you're alive, or you're dead. Either your health is full-bodied and invigorating, or you're sliding down a slippery slope.

Either you're a vegan, or you're not. We are infinitesimal and God is infinite. We are sinful and God is holy, holy, holy. We are (often) the heartless tyrants of non-human animals, and non-human animals are our innocent companions.

When something like veganism is presented to us, it's up to us not to simply shrug it off and pretend like it's another urban trend, but to examine it for what it's worth. If veganism *really is* what it claims to be – a lifestyle oriented around the holistic removal of suffering and compassion for all – it either is or is not a hoax.

A movement that makes such a bold and sweeping claim has no room – similarly to

Christianity – to be only partly right. It's either a total sham, devoid of science, sound logic and inherent truth, or it's completely correct, and people will rail against it until the majority accepts and embraces it.

The Call To Christian Justice

There's constantly talk among Christian circles about what the best uses of resources are. It's often straightforward and simple to recognize how much God blesses us with, so this is often not the point of contention.

Where Christians usually get hung up – especially amongst each other – is how far to go, or what areas to explore when stewardship and justice are concerned. Many of us want to do what we hear our pastors and teachers recommending us to do. And this is not a bad thing – if a pastor has taken time and energy to deeply consider a rightful course of action for fellow Christians to embark on, it is worth listening to their words.

The problem begins when Christians attend church on Sunday, do the recommended action, and call it a day. In other words, we build for ourselves a convenient bubble of safety and complacency by only taking and doing what other people recommend for us. The human desire to absorb information from experts is appropriate but it can undermine efforts to truly move things forward in the way they need to move forward.

Christians must be boldly active in using resources for maximum impact and effectiveness. What does this mean? It usually means asking ourselves a handful of critical questions before, during and after any sort of use of resources:

BEFORE:

- What is the desired objective of this activity or event?
- What kind of resources do we need?
- Who is in charge of resource expenditures and allocations?
- How much time do we have to prepare for the use of said resources?
- What kind of result(s) do we want?
- Are we modeling this event after any kind of successful prior event?

DURING:

- Are resources being used appropriately?
- Is there a surplus or shortage of resources?
- What is the most valuable resource here? Is it being used effectively?
- What is the least valuable resource here? Is it being allocated properly and/or downsized?

AFTER:

- Were resources used effectively?
- What means did we use to measure resource expenditures?
- Did we end up with a surplus of any kind?
- What was the result of a surplus or ineffective use?
- How well were all the resources used?
- Were we missing a resource?

- What ultimate role did the resources play in the success or failure of the event/activity?
- What would we have done differently?
- What will we do differently next time, if applicable?

The point in all of this, far and above anything else, is stewardship. To use resources effectively and properly, we must follow the above framework of steps and always examine the position of our heart as we do so.

How To Ignite Change

The world is moving too quickly for Christians to only "do what has worked previously." This is a cop-out mindset that only props up comfort and ease. Christianity is about bringing love, truth, justice and compassion into the world at all costs – not merely the places and times that "feel" right or seem easy enough.

We must be relentless innovators towards good. The essence of good can be defined nearly identically to that of Dennis Prager's quote at the beginning of this book. Goodness consists not of what feels right or seems right, but what produces actual *good results*. In other words, the personal sacrifices necessary to achieve good cannot be constrained by how much individual satisfaction or protection of comfort a person or group posits as necessary.

Religions and movements of all kinds were started by small groups of radical believers who took massive action. We must continue to uphold that. We cannot be content with simply putting on a mask and making things look good.

Christians must be concerned with how to represent grace, love, truth and justice in every area of our lives, not just the ones our parents and grandparents interacted with. In his unique work *For Love Of Animals,* Charles Camosy shares the idea that true justice is deeply inquisitive and consistent.

Christians cannot pray for opportunities to exemplify love and then avoid real-life opportunities to truly **love**. It *will* hurt many times, but we must be living, breathing examples of people who back up words with actions.

Non-human animal enslavement is so systemic and deeply rooted that we cannot reasonably ignore it on any account. It is easy for us to look at the plights of non-human animals and quickly brush them aside, considering them entirely unworthy of concern or at the very least, a problem to be investigated and a cause to be championed "some day."

We must be focused on uprooting evil at its core, not simply hacking at the branches. "This problem is too huge" is not a valid excuse for anything. If we truly believe God is bigger than any problem, we must live like it.

Chapter 9 Thesis:

As effective as veganism is in solving most of the world's ills, not everyone will be receptive to this solution, and this includes Christians. Individuals who have latched onto the viability, truth and consummate adequacy of veganism must be gracefully patient with and firmly loving of those who oppose veganism or outrightly defy it. This attitude also applies to individuals who are indifferent towards veganism, though a case-by-case approach must be taken with those who don't have clear stances on veganism yet.

Additionally, Christians who are vegan or approaching veganism must understand that most people will regard the vegan movement today as most people looked at the abolition movement hundreds of years or even decades ago. The public generally does not think veganism makes sense or is worthwhile, if they are even paying attention in the first place. Those committed to veganism must be respectfully analytical of leaders, teachers, legal authorities and other influential figures who speak of revering love and justice but may be lacking in optimal behaviors. Vegans and those seeking justice can then appropriately engage non-vegans in open-handed discussion that, when executed respectfully and thoroughly, results in both sides walking away more informed and a vegan world that much closer to fruition.

"Knowledge comes, but wisdom lingers. It may not be difficult to store up in the mind a vast quantity of facts within a comparatively short time, but the ability to form judgments requires the severe discipline of hard work and the tempering heat of experience and maturity." – Calvin Coolidge

Chapter 10: Working With One Another In Christ's Grace

"The mouths of the righteous utter wisdom, and their tongues speak what is just." – Psalm 37:30, NIV

We Christians desire and strive for goodness in the past, present and future. As Christians, we must be willing to examine statements and movements from a Christian lens, not merely a personal or cultural one. We must cling to justice, truth, love, sacrifice and hope above all other cultural comforts.

With all actions we take, we must ask ourselves:

- Is this something Jesus would have done?
- Does this advance Christian values?
- Does this advance good for the group in question?
- Does this advance good for humans?

After all, Christian morals and secular morals aren't different on the surface – it's in one's actions that reality truly surfaces.

As Christians, we should not be on the outskirts of justice, sacrifice, politics and world change – we should be the very faces and names championing these realms.

By now, we've covered the fundamentals of why veganism is critical, how it works, why Christianity should wholeheartedly embrace it and how to further structure it into our lives.

This leaves one question:

How do we create a framework for a livable future?

This chapter is devoted to mindsets, questions and prompts that can help us all benefit. This chapter will provide material for Christian vegans who want to share this message with those close to them, as well as material for Christians who are considering veganism but still have questions about it.

If you're a Christian who has already gone vegan, please check out the questions below:

- Why did I go vegan originally? Am I at a place where I'm comfortable sharing this information with others?

_____

_____

_____

_____

- What is my primary conviction or reason for becoming a vegan?

_____

_____

_____

_____

- Is veganism identity-level for me, or not? Why is this?

_____

_____

_____

_____

- Have I incorporated my vegan convictions into my faith, and visa versa? Why or why not?

_____

_____

_____

_____

- Do I feel comfortable sharing with others about how Christianity can naturally and wholeheartedly embrace veganism?

_____

_____

_____

_____

If you're a Christian who has been presented with veganism but still has questions about it, check out the questions below:

- How has veganism been presented to me?

_____

_____

_____

_____

- Has it been effective? Why or why not?

_____

_____

_____

_____

- Do I have any questions remaining about veganism?

_____

_____

_____

- Is there something that bothers me about the premise of veganism? What is it?

_____

_____

_____

- Is there anything that doesn't make sense? What is it, and how may I go about researching that?

_____

_____

_____

- Am I afraid of missing out on a food? What food is this?

_____

_____

_____

- Do my Christian values overlap with vegan values?

_____

_____

_____

_____

- Does veganism make sense from an environmental standpoint?

_____

_____

_____

_____

- Does veganism make sense from a non-human animal standpoint?

_____

_____

_____

- Does veganism make sense from a personal health standpoint?

_____

_____

_____

_____

- Does veganism make sense from a holistic justice standpoint?

_____

_____

_____

_____

Chapter 10 Thesis:

At the end of the day, words only matter some; it is actions that carry the torch. It is the Christian vegan's job to speak to fellow Christians about the viability of veganism, as well as seek out friendly but truthful conversations with non-Christians about their own convictions and beliefs. Values must be translated into actions, and actions must be transformed into habits. Only through such a pattern can Christians more fully and appropriately represent justice and help create a peaceful, just world that respects and loves all creatures.

"I have found it advisable not to give too much heed to what people say when I am trying to accomplish something of consequence. Invariably they proclaim it can't be done. I deem that the very best time to make the effort." – Calvin Coolidge

Conclusion: Why Does All Of This Matter?

There's a possibility that even after reading this book, your thoughts go something along the lines of:

- They're just animals anyways; what's the big deal?
- I'm not a farmer or anything; I don't see how this personally affects me, or is my problem to handle.
- I'm content with my cat/dog/other pet; why do I need to be friends with all these other animals?
- I get your points Brad, and I agree, but don't you think this is an impossible goal?
- I care, but what if other people don't care?
- My friends and family are going to think I'm insane, and I don't want to risk ruining my relationships with them.
- This is a worthwhile goal but it's just so unrealistic; I'm going to fail at some point/other people are going to give up at some point. Why bother?

These are all valid questions. As much as I would love to answer all of these questions in depth in this book, I have decided to field questions like these on Quora. You can always check out my Quora profile for my latest answers on general vegan questions. For the sake of this book though, and to offer my best singular response to the questions above, I offer these thoughts:

Consider how spending some time in pure, breathtaking nature rejuvenates the mind, body, heart and soul.

Consider how full of life you feel when getting the chance to touch and become close to a non-human animal that is not part of your daily life.

Consider how much pop culture enjoys and appreciates seeing non-human animals of all kinds being free to live their lives, untainted and unrestrained by human greed and corruption.

Consider how fresh and alive you feel when you eat well, sleep deeply, drink plenty of water, exercise and avoid junk foods.

Consider how utterly grateful you feel when your actions produce goodness and joy in the lives of others.

Resources by Brad Johnson

Learn more about websites, blog posts, educational resources, professional information and other works from the author:

Main Website –
http://bradleyjohnsonproductions.com/

Lose Fat Rapidly: 8 Simple Steps To Drop Fat On A Vegan Diet –
https://www.amazon.com/Lose-Fat-Rapidly-Simple-Steps-ebook/dp/B01N08FQH3/

Amazon Author Page –
https://www.amazon.com/Brad-Johnson/e/B010WNX9H0/

Quora Answers and Posts –
https://www.quora.com/profile/Brad-Johnson-61

Lifehack Articles –
http://www.lifehack.org/author/brad-johnson

Recommended Reading

- *Mind If I Order The Cheeseburger? And Other Questions People Ask Vegans,* by Sherry Colb
- *Meat Logic: Why Do We Eat Animals?* by Charles Horn
- *For Love Of Animals: Christian Ethics, Consistent Action* by Charles Camosy
- *Dominion: The Power Of Man, The Suffering Of Animals, And The Call To Mercy* by Matthew Scully
- *Eating Animals* by Jonathan Foer
- *A Faith Embracing All Creatures* by Multiple Authors
- *Is God A Vegetarian?* by Andrew Linzey
- *The First Step* by Leo Tolstoy

Bonus Book And Review Reminder

Dear *Justice Is Served* readers,

As a thank you for picking up a copy of the book I'd like to give you one of my Top 15-Selling Kindle books, *Lose Fat Rapidly*, free...

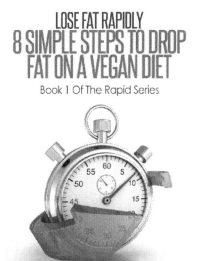

To obtain your free copy just go here:
http://rapidseries.s3.amazonaws.com/Lose+Fat+Rap idly+V4.pdf

Also, as a quick reminder! If you enjoyed *Justice Is Served* – or even if you didn't – I

welcome your review on Amazon! Please consider leaving your thoughts on the *Justice Is Served* Amazon book page, even if it's just two or three sentences. Your review helps other readers decide what to read!

All the very best,
Brad Johnson

Works Cited

Adams, Carol J. "The Sexual Politics of Meat." *Carol J. Adams*. Bloomsbury Academic, 2015. Web. 15 Jan. 2017. <http://caroljadams.com/spom-the-book/>.

Akers, Keith. "The Fish Stories in the New Testament." *Compassionate Spirit*. Compassionate Spirit, 31 Jan. 2012. Web. 04 Mar. 2017. <http://www.compassionatespirit.com/wpblog/2012/01/31/the-fish-stories-in-the-new-testament/>.

Akers, Keith. "Pearls Before Swine." *Compassionate Spirit*. Compassionate Spirit, 11 Mar. 2011. Web. 04 Mar. 2017. <http://www.compassionatespirit.com/wpblog/2011/03/11/pearls-before-swine/>.

Akers, Keith. "Religion and Vegetarianism — Some Surprising Results." *Compassionate Spirit*. Compassionate Spirit, 16 Aug. 2010. Web. 04 Mar. 2017. <http://www.compassionatespirit.com/wpblog/2010/08/16/religion-and-vegetarianism-%E2%80%94-some-surprising-results/>.

Akers, Keith. "Was Jesus a Vegetarian?" *Compassionate Spirit*. Compassionate Spirit, 1 Dec. 2015. Web. 04 Mar. 2017.

<http://www.compassionatespirit.com/wpblog/2015/12/01/was-jesus-a-vegetarian/>.

ALDF. "Animal Fighting Case Study: Michael Vick." *Animal Legal Defense Fund*. Animal Legal Defense Fund, 2007. Web. 04 Mar. 2017. <http://aldf.org/resources/laws-cases/animal-fighting-case-study-michael-vick/>.

ALDF. "No Boundaries for Abusers: The Link Between Cruelty to Animals and Violence Toward Humans." *Animal Legal Defense Fund*. Animal Legal Defense Fund, 2015. Web. 04 Mar. 2017. <http://aldf.org/resources/when-your-companion-animal-has-been-harmed/no-boundaries-for-abusers-the-link-between-cruelty-to-animals-and-violence-toward-humans/>.

Baumel, Syd. "Veganism and the Major World Religions." *Veganism and the Major World Religions*. Society of Ethical and Religious Vegetarians, 2005. Web. 04 Mar. 2017. <http://serv-online.org/pamphlet2005.htm>.

Chatham, Michael. "Could Veganism End World Hunger?" *Gentle World — Reaching out for over 40 Years, to Inspire the Vegan in Everyone*. Gentle World, 1 Sept. 2014. Web. 15 Jan. 2017. <http://gentleworld.org/could-veganism-end-world-hunger/>.

Chrispeels, Maarten. "Robot Check." *Robot Check*. Jones & Bartlett, Mar. 1994. Web. 15 Jan. 2017. <http://www.amazon.com/Plants-Genes-

Agriculture-Maarten-
Chrispeels/dp/0867208716>.

Chrissy. "90% of Serial Killers Admit To Killing
Animals Before Killing
Humans." *Psych2Go.net*. Psych2Go.net, 02
Sept. 2014. Web. 04 Mar. 2017.
<https://www.psych2go.net/90-of-serial-
killers-admit-to-killing-animals-before-killing-
humans/>.

Daniel, Carrie R., Amanda J. Cross, Corinna
Koebnick, and Rashmi Sinha. "Trends in Meat
Consumption in the United States." *Public
Health Nutrition*. U.S. National Library of
Medicine, Apr. 2011. Web. 04 Mar. 2017.
<https://www.ncbi.nlm.nih.gov/pmc/articles/
PMC3045642/>.

Dasa, Dr. Sahadeva. "Article Headline." *ISKCON
News*. ISKCON News, 02 Mar. 2016. Web. 15
Jan. 2017. <http://iskconnews.org/meat-
eating-the-cause-for-world-hunger-criminal-
waste-of-grains,3607/>.

Ferraro, Ken. "Study Finds Some Faithful Less Likely
to Pass the Plate." *Study Finds Some Faithful
Less Likely to Pass the Plate*. Purdue
University, 24 Aug. 2006. Web. 04 Mar. 2017.
<http://www.purdue.edu/uns/html4ever/2006
/060824.Ferraro.obesity.html>.

Gerbens-Leenes, P. W., M. M. Mekonnen, and A. Y.
Hoekstra. "The Water Footprint of Poultry,
Pork and Beef: A Comparative Study in
Different Countries and Production

Systems." *The Water Footprint of Poultry, Pork and Beef: A Comparative Study in Different Countries and Production Systems.* Water Resources and Industry, Mar. 2013. Web. 15 Jan. 2017. <http://www.sciencedirect.com/science/article/pii/S2212371713000024>.

Gimenez, Eric Holt. "We Already Grow Enough Food For 10 Billion People -- and Still Can't End Hunger." *The Huffington Post.* TheHuffingtonPost.com, 2 May 2012. Web. 15 Jan. 2017. <http://www.huffingtonpost.com/eric-holt-gimenez/world-hunger_b_1463429.html>.

Goodby, Jeff. "20 Years of 'Got Milk?'" *Adweek.* Adweek, 25 Oct. 2013. Web. 04 Mar. 2017. <http://www.adweek.com/creativity/20-years-got-milk-153399/>.

Greenwood, Arin. "Pigs Are Highly Social And Really Smart. So, Um, About Eating Them..." *The Huffington Post.* TheHuffingtonPost.com, 15 June 2015. Web. 04 Mar. 2017. <http://www.huffingtonpost.com/2015/06/15/are-pigs-intelligent_n_7585582.html>.

Grissom, Stacie. "These Were Michael Vick's Fighting Dogs. Where They Are Now Is Beautiful." *BarkPost.* BarkPost, 26 Aug. 2015. Web. 04 Mar. 2017. <http://stories.barkpost.com/vicktory-dogs/>.

Hadley, Billie. "Is a Vegetarian Diet Actually Cheaper?" *LearnVest.* LearnVest, 21 Oct. 2010.

Web. 04 Mar. 2017.
<https://www.learnvest.com/knowledge-center/do-vegetarians-save-money/#pid-2775_aint-0>.

Hadley, Billie. "Is a Vegetarian Diet Actually Cheaper?" *LearnVest*. LearnVest, 21 Oct. 2010. Web. 15 Jan. 2017. <https://www.learnvest.com/knowledge-center/do-vegetarians-save-money/#pid-2775_aint-0>.

Harish. "Meat Consumption Patterns by Race and Gender." *Counting Animals*. Counting Animals, 23 Aug. 2012. Web. 04 Mar. 2017. <http://www.countinganimals.com/meat-consumption-patterns-by-race-and-gender/>.

Human Animal Liberation. "ROOTS OF OPPRESSION." *Human Animal Liberation*. Http://human-animal-liberation.blogspot.com/2009/06/roots-of-oppression.html, 2015. Web. 04 Mar. 2017. <http://human-animal-liberation.blogspot.com/2009/06/roots-of-oppression.html>.

Human Animal Liberation. "ROOTS OF OPPRESSION." *Human Animal Liberation*. Human Animal Liberation, 2006. Web. 15 Jan. 2017. <http://human-animal-liberation.blogspot.com/2009/06/roots-of-oppression.html>.

"Latest Alzheimer's Facts and Figures." *Alzheimer's Association*. Alzheimer's Association, 29 Mar.

2016. Web. 04 Mar. 2017.
<http://www.alz.org/facts/>.

Laws, Rita. "History of Vegetarianism - Native
Americans and Vegetarianism." *History of
Vegetarianism - Native Americans and
Vegetarianism.* International Vegetarian
Union, Sept. 1994. Web. 15 Jan. 2017.
<http://www.ivu.org/history/native_american
s.html>.

Mastin, Luke. "Deconstructionism - By Movement /
School - The Basics of
Philosophy." *Deconstructionism - By
Movement / School - The Basics of Philosophy.*
The Basics of Philosophy, 2008. Web. 04 Mar.
2017.
<http://www.philosophybasics.com/movement
s_deconstructionism.html>.

Mastin, Luke. "Deconstructionism - By Movement /
School - The Basics of
Philosophy." *Deconstructionism - By
Movement / School - The Basics of Philosophy.*
Philosophy Basics, 2008. Web. 15 Jan. 2017.
<http://www.philosophybasics.com/movement
s_deconstructionism.html>.

McDermott, John, and Delia Grace. "Animal Farming
and Human Health Are Intimately Linked |
John McDermott and Delia Grace." *Poverty
Matters Blog.* Guardian News and Media, 11
Feb. 2011. Web. 15 Jan. 2017.
<http://www.theguardian.com/global-
development/poverty-

matters/2011/feb/11/animal-human-health-diseases-link-agriculture>.

Melson, PhD, Gail F. "Do Mass Killers Start Out by Harming Pets?" *Psychology Today.* Psychology Today, 20 Feb. 2013. Web. 04 Mar. 2017. <https://www.psychologytoday.com/blog/why-the-wild-things-are/201302/do-mass-killers-start-out-harming-pets>.

Mic the Vegan. "Allan Savory's 5 Big Lies - Debunked - PART 2." *YouTube.* YouTube, 20 Jan. 2016. Web. 15 Jan. 2017. <https://www.youtube.com/watch?v=Z5BqDy Drj8E>.

Mic the Vegan. "Allan Savory's 5 Big Lies - Debunked." *YouTube.* YouTube, 20 Jan. 2016. Web. 15 Jan. 2017. <https://www.youtube.com/watch?v=_EDpuQ MpyYw>.

Mic the Vegan. "Vegan Earth vs. Earth: Aliens Are Placing Bets." *YouTube.* YouTube, 28 Aug. 2015. Web. 15 Jan. 2017. <https://www.youtube.com/watch?v=grUOpZo Clqo>.

National Link Coalition. "How Are Animal Abuse and Family Violence Linked? |." *National Link Coalition.* National Link Coalition, 2013. Web. 04 Mar. 2017. <http://nationallinkcoalition.org/faqs/what-is-the-link>.

National Soybean Research Laboratory. "Benefits of
    Soy." *Benefits of Soy | National Soybean
    Research Laboratory*. NSRL, 2016. Web. 15
    Jan. 2017.
    <http://nsrl.illinois.edu/content/benefits-soy>.

Newkirk, Ingrid. "9 Ways Pigs Are Smarter Than Your
    Honor Student." *The Huffington Post*.
    TheHuffingtonPost.com, 15 Apr. 2014. Web. 04
    Mar. 2017.
    <http://www.huffingtonpost.com/ingrid-
    newkirk/9-ways-pigs-are-smarter-
    t_b_5154321.html>.

NY Daily News. "Alzheimer's Kills Many More than
    Previously Thought: Study." *NY Daily News*.
    NY Daily News, 06 Mar. 2014. Web. 04 Mar.
    2017. <http://www.nydailynews.com/life-
    style/health/alzheimer-kills-previously-
    thought-study-article-1.1712078>.

Open Bible. "88 Bible Verses about New Heavens And
    New Earth." *What Does the Bible Say About
    New Heavens And New Earth?* Open Bible,
    2016. Web. 15 Jan. 2017.

Oppenlander, Richard. "Blog." *Comfortably Unaware
    :: The World Hunger-Food Choice Connection:
    A Summary*. Comfortably Unaware, 22 Apr.
    2012. Web. 15 Jan. 2017.
    <http://comfortablyunaware.com/blog/the-
    world-hunger-food-choice-connection-a-
    summary/>.

Pachniewska, Amanda. "List of Animals That Have
    Passed the Mirror Test." *Animal Cognition*.

Animal Cognition, 29 Oct. 2016. Web. 15 Jan. 2017.

PETA. "Vegans Save 198 Animals a Year." *PETA*. PETA, 02 May 2016. Web. 04 Mar. 2017. <http://www.peta.org/blog/vegans-save-185-animals-year/>.

PETA. "Vegans Save 198 Animals a Year." *PETA*. PETA, 02 May 2016. Web. 15 Jan. 2017. <http://www.peta.org/blog/vegans-save-185-animals-year/>.

Philpott, Tom. "The American Diet in One Chart, with Lots of Fats and Sugars." *Grist*. Grist, 06 Apr. 2011. Web. 04 Mar. 2017. <http://grist.org/industrial-agriculture/2011-04-05-american-diet-one-chart-lots-of-fats-sugars/>.

Philpott, Tom. "The Standard American Diet in 3 Simple Charts." *Mother Jones*. Mother Jones, 20 Jan. 2014. Web. 04 Mar. 2017. <http://www.motherjones.com/tom-philpott/2014/01/standard-american-diet-sad-charts>.

Pimentel, David, and Marcia Pimentel. "Sustainability of Meat-based and Plant-based Diets and the Environment1,2,3." *American Society for Clinical Nutrition*. American Society for Clinical Nutrition, 01 Sept. 2003. Web. 04 Mar. 2017. <http://ajcn.nutrition.org/content/78/3/660S.full>.

Premack, Rachel. "Meat Is Horrible." *The Washington Post*. WP Company, 03 July 2016. Web. 04 Mar. 2017. <https://www.washingtonpost.com/news/wonk/wp/2016/06/30/how-meat-is-destroying-the-planet-in-seven-charts/?utm_term=.f30d70e3c802&wpisrc=nl_wemost-draw4&wpmm=1>.

Premack, Rachel. "Meat Is Horrible." *The Washington Post*. WP Company, 3 July 2016. Web. 15 Jan. 2017. <https://www.washingtonpost.com/news/wonk/wp/2016/06/30/how-meat-is-destroying-the-planet-in-seven-charts/?wpisrc=nl_wemost-draw4&wpmm=1>.

Rabbit, Vegan. "People For the Ethical Treatment of Plants: 4 Reasons Why the "Plant Sentience" Argument Doesn't Work." *Vegan Rabbit*. Vegan Rabbit, 23 Nov. 2013. Web. 15 Jan. 2017. <https://veganrabbit.com/2013/03/18/plant-sentience-and-pain/>.

Rainer, Thom. "Fourteen Symptoms of Toxic Church Leaders." *ThomRainer.com*. Thom Rainer, 01 Oct. 2014. Web. 15 Jan. 2017. <http://thomrainer.com/2014/10/fourteen-symptoms-toxic-church-leaders/>.

Rainer, Thom S. "Fourteen Symptoms of Toxic Church Leaders." *ThomRainer.com*. ThomRainer.com, 01 Oct. 2014. Web. 04 Mar. 2017. <http://thomrainer.com/2014/10/fourteen-symptoms-toxic-church-leaders/>.

Ranker. "10 Serial Killers Who Abused Animals First." *Ranker*. Ranker, 2010. Web. 04 Mar. 2017. <http://www.ranker.com/list/serial-killers-who-abused-animals/ranker-crime?utm_expid=16418821-253.BAWaw7_5T3qAVTf7EdWDtA.0&utm_ref errer=https%3A%2F%2Fwww.google.com%2F>
.

SERV. "Veganism and the Major World Religions." *Veganism and the Major World Religions.* Society of Ethical and Religious Vegetarians, 2005. Web. 15 Jan. 2017. <http://serv-online.org/pamphlet2005.htm>.

Shapiro, Paul. "Americans Are Eating Less and Less Meat Every Year. Why?" *Forks Over Knives.* Forks Over Knives, 03 June 2016. Web. 04 Mar. 2017. <https://www.forksoverknives.com/americans-are-eating-less-and-less-meat-every-year-why/>.

Smil, Vaclav. "Harvesting the Biosphere: The Human Impact." *Population and Development Review* 37.4 (2011): 613-36. *Vaclav Smil.* Vaclav Smil, Dec. 2011. Web. 15 Jan. 2017. <http://www.vaclavsmil.com/wp-content/uploads/PDR37-4.Smil_.pgs613-636.pdf>.

Sun, Eryn. "Firm Faith, Fat Body? Study Finds High Rate of Obesity among Religious." *The Christian Post*. The Christian Post, 24 Mar. 2011. Web. 04 Mar. 2017.

<http://www.christianpost.com/news/firm-faith-fat-body-study-finds-high-rate-of-obesity-among-religious-49568/>.

Thornton, Philip, Mario Herrero, and Polly Ericksen. "Https://cgspace.cgiar.org/bitstream/handle/10568/10601/IssueBrief3.pdf." *International Livestock Research Institute* (2011): n. pag. Nov. 2011. Web. 3 Mar. 2017. <https://cgspace.cgiar.org/bitstream/handle/10568/10601/IssueBrief3.pdf>.

Tina. "Global Hunger: The More Meat We Eat, the Fewer People We Can Feed | Earthoria." *Global Hunger: The More Meat We Eat, the Fewer People We Can Feed | Earthoria*. Earthoria, 25 Mar. 2008. Web. 15 Jan. 2017. <http://www.earthoria.com/global-hunger-the-more-meat-we-eat-the-fewer-people-we-can-feed.html>.

Trauth, Erin. "Is 2014 the Year of the Vegan?" *One Green Planet*. One Green Planet, 16 Jan. 2014. Web. 15 Jan. 2017. <http://www.onegreenplanet.org/news/is-2014-the-year-of-the-vegan/>.

Tuttle, Will. "Circles of Compassion: Essays Connecting Issues of Justice Paperback – January 1, 2015." *Circles of Compassion: Essays Connecting Issues of Justice: Will Tuttle, Robin Ridley / Parfait Studio: 9781940184067: Amazon.com: Books*. Vegan Publishers, 2015. Web. 15 Jan. 2017. <http://www.amazon.com/Circles-

Compassion-Essays-Connecting-Justice/dp/1940184061>.

Werder, Ed. "Apologetic Vick Gets 23-month Sentence on Dogfighting Charges." *ESPN.* ESPN Internet Ventures, 11 Dec. 2007. Web. 04 Mar. 2017. <http://www.espn.com/nfl/news/story?id=314 8549>.
Wikipedia. "Got Milk?" *Wikipedia.* Wikimedia Foundation, 24 Feb. 2017. Web. 04 Mar. 2017. <https://en.wikipedia.org/wiki/Got_Milk%3F >.

Woods, Cathleen. "The Standard American Diet Is Killing You." *Vegan Nutritionista.* Vegan Nutritionista, 2015. Web. 04 Mar. 2017. <http://www.vegan-nutritionista.com/standard-american-diet.html>.

Woods, Cathleen. "The Standard American Diet Is Killing You." *Vegan Nutritionista.* Vegan Nutritionista, 2015. Web. 15 Jan. 2017. <http://www.vegan-nutritionista.com/standard-american-diet.html>.

Yourofsky, Gary. "More Than 150 Billion Animals Slaughtered Every Year." *The Animal Kill Counter.* ADAPTT, 2010. Web. 15 Jan. 2017. <http://www.adaptt.org/killcounter.html>.

Made in the USA
Lexington, KY
03 May 2017